THE LETTERS OF SAINT PAUL
TO THE THESSALONIANS,
TIMOTHY,
AND TITUS

THE IGNATIUS CATHOLIC STUDY BIBLE

REVISED STANDARD VERSION
SECOND CATHOLIC EDITION

THE LETTERS OF SAINT PAUL TO THE THESSALONIANS, TIMOTHY, AND TITUS

With Introduction, Commentary, and Notes

by

Scott Hahn and Curtis Mitch

and

with Study Questions by

Dennis Walters

IGNATIUS PRESS   SAN FRANCISCO

Published with ecclesiastical approval.

Original RSV Bible text:
Nihil obstat: Thomas Hanlon, S.T.L., L.S.S., Ph.L.
Imprimatur: + Peter W. Bertholome, D.D.
Bishop of Saint Cloud, Minnesota
May 11, 1966

Second Catholic Edition approved under the same *imprimatur* by the
Secretariat for Doctrine and Pastoral Practices,
National Conference of Catholic Bishops
February 29, 2000

Introduction, commentaries, and notes:
Nihil obstat: Rev. Msgr. J. Warren Holleran, S.T.D.
Imprimatur: + Most Reverend George Niederauer
Archbishop of San Francisco
July 24, 2006

This *nihil obstat* and *imprimatur* are official declarations that a book or pamphlet is free of doctrinal
or moral error. No implication is contained therein that those who have granted the *nihil obstat* and
imprimatur agree with the contents, opinions, or statements expressed.

Second Catholic Edition approved by the
National Council of the Churches of Christ in the USA

Cover art: Paolo Veronese (1528–1588)
Resurrection of Christ
Kunsthistorisches Museum, Vienna, Austria
Erich Lessing / Art Resource, N.Y.

Cover design by Riz Boncan Marsella

Published by Ignatius Press in 2006
Bible text: Revised Standard Version, Second Catholic Edition
© 2006 by the Division of Christian Education of the
National Council of the Churches of Christ in the United States of America
All rights reserved

Introductions, commentaries, notes, headings, and study questions
© 2006, Ignatius Press, San Francisco
All rights reserved
ISBN 978-1-58617-162-9
ISBN 1-58617-162-3
Printed in the United States of America ∞

CONTENTS

INTRODUCTION TO THE IGNATIUS STUDY BIBLE

You are approaching the "word of God". This is the title Christians most commonly give to the Bible, and the expression is rich in meaning. It is also the title given to the Second Person of the Blessed Trinity, God the Son. For Jesus Christ became flesh for our salvation, and "the name by which he is called is The Word of God" (Rev 19:13; cf. Jn 1:14).

The word of God is Scripture. The Word of God is Jesus. This close association between God's *written* word and his *eternal* Word is intentional and has been the custom of the Church since the first generation. "All Sacred Scripture is but one book, and this one book is Christ, 'because all divine Scripture speaks of Christ, and all divine Scripture is fulfilled in Christ'[1]" (CCC 134). This does not mean that the Scriptures are divine in the same way that Jesus is divine. They are, rather, divinely inspired and, as such, are unique in world literature, just as the Incarnation of the eternal Word is unique in human history.

Yet we can say that the inspired word resembles the incarnate Word in several important ways. Jesus Christ is the Word of God incarnate. In his humanity, he is like us in all things, except for sin. As a work of man, the Bible is like any other book, except without error. Both Christ and Scripture, says the Second Vatican Council, are given "for the sake of our salvation" (*Dei Verbum* 11), and both give us God's definitive revelation of himself. We cannot, therefore, conceive of one without the other: the Bible without Jesus, or Jesus without the Bible. Each is the interpretive key to the other. And because Christ is the subject of all the Scriptures, St. Jerome insists, "Ignorance of the Scriptures is ignorance of Christ"[2] (CCC 133).

When we approach the Bible, then, we approach Jesus, the Word of God; and in order to encounter Jesus, we must approach him in a prayerful study of the inspired word of God, the Sacred Scriptures.

Inspiration and Inerrancy The Catholic Church makes mighty claims for the Bible, and our acceptance of those claims is essential if we are to read the Scriptures and apply them to our lives as the Church intends. So it is not enough merely to nod at words like "inspired", "unique", or "inerrant". We have to understand what the Church means by these terms, and we have to make that understanding our own. After all, what we believe about the Bible will inevitably influence the way we read the Bible. The way we read the Bible, in turn, will determine what we "get out" of its sacred pages.

These principles hold true no matter what we read: a news report, a search warrant, an advertisement, a paycheck, a doctor's prescription, an eviction notice. How (or whether) we read these things depends largely upon our preconceived notions about the reliability and authority of their sources—and the potential they have for affecting our lives. In some cases, to misunderstand a document's authority can lead to dire consequences. In others, it can keep us from enjoying rewards that are rightfully ours. In the case of the Bible, both the rewards and the consequences involved take on an ultimate value.

What does the Church mean, then, when she affirms the words of St. Paul: "All Scripture is inspired by God" (2 Tim 3:16)? Since the term "inspired" in this passage could be translated "God-breathed", it follows that God breathed forth his word in the Scriptures as you and I breathe forth air when we speak. This means that God is the primary author of the Bible. He certainly employed human authors in this task as well, but he did not merely assist them while they wrote or subsequently approve what they had written. God the Holy Spirit is the *principal* author of Scripture, while the human writers are *instrumental* authors. These human authors freely wrote everything, and only those things, that God wanted: the word of God in the very words of God. This miracle of dual authorship extends to the whole of Scripture, and to every one of its parts, so that whatever the human authors affirm, God likewise affirms through their words.

The principle of biblical inerrancy follows logically from this principle of divine authorship. After all, God cannot lie, and he cannot make mistakes. Since the Bible is divinely inspired, it must be without error in everything that its divine and human authors affirm to be true. This means that biblical inerrancy is a mystery even broader in scope than infallibility, which guarantees for us that the Church will always teach the truth concerning faith and morals. Of course the mantle of inerrancy likewise covers faith and morals, but it extends even farther to ensure that all the facts and events of salvation history are accurately presented for us in the Scriptures. Inerrancy is our guarantee that the words and deeds of God found in the Bible are unified and true, declaring with one voice the wonders of his saving love.

---

[1] Hugh of St. Victor, *De arca Noe* 2, 8: PL 176, 642: cf. ibid. 2, 9: PL 176, 642–43.
[2] *DV* 25; cf. Phil 3:8 and St. Jerome, *Commentariorum Isaiam libri xviii*, prol.: PL 24, 17b.

The guarantee of inerrancy does not mean, however, that the Bible is an all-purpose encyclopedia of information covering every field of study. The Bible is not, for example, a textbook in the empirical sciences, and it should not be treated as one. When biblical authors relate facts of the natural order, we can be sure they are speaking in a purely descriptive and "phenomenological" way, according to the way things appeared to their senses.

Biblical Authority Implicit in these doctrines is God's desire to make himself known to the world and to enter a loving relationship with every man, woman, and child he has created. God gave us the Scriptures not just to inform or motivate us; more than anything he wants to save us. This higher purpose underlies every page of the Bible, indeed every word of it.

In order to reveal himself, God used what theologians call "accommodation". Sometimes the Lord stoops down to communicate by "condescension"—that is, he speaks as humans speak, as if he had the same passions and weakness that we do (for example, God says he was "sorry" that he made man in Genesis 6:6). Other times he communicates by "elevation"—that is, by endowing human words with divine power (for example, through the prophets). The numerous examples of divine accommodation in the Bible are an expression of God's wise and fatherly ways. For a sensitive father can speak with his children either by condescension, as in baby talk, or by elevation, by bringing a child's understanding up to a more mature level.

God's word is thus saving, fatherly, and personal. Because it speaks directly to us, we must never be indifferent to its content; after all, the word of God is at once the object, cause, and support of our faith. It is, in fact, a test of our faith, since we see in the Scriptures only what faith disposes us to see. If we believe what the Church believes, we will see in Scripture the saving, inerrant, and divinely authored revelation of the Father. If we believe otherwise, we see another book altogether.

This test applies not only to rank-and-file believers but also to the Church's theologians and hierarchy, and even the Magisterium. Vatican II has stressed in recent times that Scripture must be "the very soul of sacred theology" (*Dei Verbum* 24). As Joseph Cardinal Ratzinger, Pope Benedict XVI echoed this powerful teaching with his own, insisting that, "The *normative theologians* are the authors of Holy Scripture" (emphasis added). He reminded us that Scripture and the Church's dogmatic teaching are tied tightly together, to the point of being inseparable: "Dogma is by definition nothing other than an interpretation of Scripture." The defined dogmas of our faith, then, encapsulate the Church's infallible interpretation of Scripture, and theology is a further reflection upon that work.

The Senses of Scripture Because the Bible has both divine and human authors, we are required to master a different sort of reading than we are used to. First, we must read Scripture according to its *literal* sense, as we read any other human literature. At this initial stage, we strive to discover the meaning of the words and expressions used by the biblical writers as they were understood in their original setting and by their original recipients. This means, among other things, that we do not interpret everything we read "literalistically", as though Scripture never speaks in a figurative or symbolic way (it often does!). Rather, we read it according to the rules that govern its different literary forms of writing, depending on whether we are reading a narrative, a poem, a letter, a parable, or an apocalyptic vision. The Church calls us to read the divine books in this way to ensure that we understand what the human authors were laboring to explain to God's people.

The literal sense, however, is not the only sense of Scripture, since we interpret its sacred pages according to the *spiritual* senses as well. In this way, we search out what the Holy Spirit is trying to tell us, beyond even what the human authors have consciously asserted. Whereas the literal sense of Scripture describes a historical reality—a fact, precept, or event—the spiritual senses disclose deeper mysteries revealed through the historical realities. What the soul is to the body, the spiritual senses are to the literal. You can distinguish them; but if you try to separate them, death immediately follows. St. Paul was the first to insist upon this and warn of its consequences: "God ... has qualified us to be ministers of a new covenant, not in a written code but in the Spirit; for the written code kills, but the Spirit gives life" (2 Cor 3:5–6).

Catholic tradition recognizes three spiritual senses that stand upon the foundation of the literal sense of Scripture (see CCC 115). **(1)** The first is the *allegorical* sense, which unveils the spiritual and prophetic meaning of biblical history. Allegorical interpretations thus reveal how persons, events, and institutions of Scripture can point beyond themselves toward greater mysteries yet to come (OT), or display the fruits of mysteries already revealed (NT). Christians have often read the Old Testament in this way to discover how the mystery of Christ in the New Covenant was once hidden in the Old, and how the full significance of the Old Covenant was finally made manifest in the New. Allegorical significance is likewise latent in the New Testament, especially in the life and deeds of Jesus recorded in the Gospels. Because Christ is the Head of the Church and the source of her spiritual life, what was accomplished in Christ the Head during his earthly life prefigures what he continually produces in his members through grace. The allegorical sense builds up the virtue of faith. **(2)** The second is the *tropological* or *moral* sense, which

reveals how the actions of God's people in the Old Testament and the life of Jesus in the New Testament prompt us to form virtuous habits in our own lives. It therefore draws from Scripture warnings against sin and vice, as well as inspirations to pursue holiness and purity. The moral sense is intended to build up the virtue of charity. **(3)** The third is the *anagogical* sense, which points upward to heavenly glory. It shows us how countless events in the Bible prefigure our final union with God in eternity, and how things that are "seen" on earth are figures of things "unseen" in heaven. Because the anagogical sense leads us to contemplate our destiny, it is meant to build up the virtue of hope. Together with the literal sense, then, these spiritual senses draw out the fullness of what God wants to give us through his Word and as such comprise what ancient tradition has called the "full sense" of Sacred Scripture.

All of this means that the deeds and events of the Bible are charged with meaning beyond what is immediately apparent to the reader. In essence, that meaning is Jesus Christ and the salvation he died to give us. This is especially true of the books of the New Testament, which proclaim Jesus explicitly; but it is also true of the Old Testament, which speaks of Jesus in more hidden and symbolic ways. The human authors of the Old Testament told us as much as they were able, but they could not clearly discern the shape of all future events standing at such a distance. It is the Bible's divine Author, the Holy Spirit, who could and did foretell the saving work of Christ, from the first page of the Book of Genesis onward.

The New Testament did not, therefore, abolish the Old. Rather, the New fulfilled the Old, and in doing so, it lifted the veil that kept hidden the face of the Lord's bride. Once the veil is removed, we suddenly see the world of the Old Covenant charged with grandeur. Water, fire, clouds, gardens, trees, hills, doves, lambs—all of these things are memorable details in the history and poetry of Israel. But now, seen in the light of Jesus Christ, they are much more. For the Christian with eyes to see, water symbolizes the saving power of Baptism; fire, the Holy Spirit; the spotless lamb, Christ crucified; Jerusalem, the city of heavenly glory.

The spiritual reading of Scripture is nothing new. Indeed the very first Christians read the Bible this way. St. Paul describes Adam as a "type" that prefigured Jesus Christ (Rom 5:14). A "type" is a real person, place, thing, or event in the Old Testament that foreshadows something greater in the New. From this term we get the word "typology", referring to the study of how the Old Testament prefigures Christ (CCC 128–30). Elsewhere St. Paul draws deeper meanings out of the story of Abraham's sons, declaring, "This is an allegory" (Gal 4:24). He is not suggesting that these events of the distant past never really happened; he is saying that the events both happened *and* signified something more glorious yet to come.

The New Testament later describes the Tabernacle of ancient Israel as "a copy and shadow of the heavenly sanctuary" (Heb 8:5) and the Mosaic Law as a "shadow of the good things to come" (Heb 10:1). St. Peter, in turn, notes that Noah and his family were "saved through water" in a way that "corresponds" to sacramental Baptism, which "now saves you" (1 Pet 3:20–21). Interestingly, the expression that is translated "corresponds" in this verse is a Greek term that denotes the fulfillment or counterpart of an ancient "type".

We need not look to the apostles, however, to justify a spiritual reading of the Bible. After all, Jesus himself read the Old Testament this way. He referred to Jonah (Mt 12:39), Solomon (Mt 12:42), the Temple (Jn 2:19), and the brazen serpent (Jn 3:14) as "signs" that pointed forward to him. We see in Luke's Gospel, as Christ comforted the disciples on the road to Emmaus, that "beginning with Moses and all the prophets, he interpreted to them in all the Scriptures the things concerning himself" (Lk 24:27). It was precisely this extensive spiritual interpretation of the Old Testament that made such an impact on these once-discouraged travelers, causing their hearts to "burn" within them (Lk 24:32).

Criteria for Biblical Interpretation   We too must learn to discern the "full sense" of Scripture as it includes both the literal and spiritual senses together. Still, this does not mean we should "read into" the Bible meanings that are not really there. Spiritual exegesis is not an unrestrained flight of the imagination. Rather, it is a sacred science that proceeds according to certain principles and stands accountable to sacred tradition, the Magisterium, and the wider community of biblical interpreters (both living and deceased).

In searching out the full sense of a text, we should always avoid the extreme tendency to "over-spiritualize" in a way that minimizes or denies the Bible's literal truth. St. Thomas Aquinas was well aware of this danger and asserted that "all other senses of Sacred Scripture are based on the literal" (*STh* I, 1, 10, *ad* 1, quoted in CCC 116). On the other hand, we should never confine the meaning of a text to the literal, intended sense of its human author, as if the divine Author did not intend the passage to be read in the light of Christ's coming.

Fortunately the Church has given us guidelines in our study of Scripture. The unique character and divine authorship of the Bible calls us to read it "in the Spirit" (*Dei Verbum* 12). Vatican II outlines this teaching in a practical way by directing us to read the Scriptures according to three specific criteria:

1. We must "[b]e especially attentive 'to the content and unity of the whole Scripture'" (CCC 112).

2. We must "[r]ead the Scripture within 'the living Tradition of the whole Church'" (CCC 113).

3. We must "[b]e attentive to the analogy of faith" (CCC 114; cf. Rom 12:6).

These criteria protect us from many of the dangers that ensnare readers of the Bible, from the newest inquirer to the most prestigious scholar. Reading Scripture out of context is one such pitfall, and probably the one most difficult to avoid. A memorable cartoon from the 1950s shows a young man poring over the pages of the Bible. He says to his sister: "Don't bother me now; I'm trying to find a Scripture verse to back up one of my preconceived notions." No doubt a biblical text pried from its context can be twisted to say something very different from what its author actually intended.

The Church's criteria guide us here by defining what constitutes the authentic "context" of a given biblical passage. The first criterion directs us to the literary context of every verse, including not only the words and paragraphs that surround it, but also the entire corpus of the biblical author's writings and, indeed, the span of the entire Bible. The *complete* literary context of any Scripture verse includes every text from Genesis to Revelation—because the Bible is a unified book, not just a library of different books. When the Church canonized the Book of Revelation, for example, she recognized it to be incomprehensible apart from the wider context of the entire Bible.

The second criterion places the Bible firmly within the context of a community that treasures a "living tradition". That community is the People of God down through the ages. Christians lived out their faith for well over a millennium before the printing press was invented. For centuries, few believers owned copies of the Gospels, and few people could read anyway. Yet they absorbed the gospel—through the sermons of their bishops and clergy, through prayer and meditation, through Christian art, through liturgical celebrations, and through oral tradition. These were expressions of the one "living tradition", a culture of living faith that stretches from ancient Israel to the contemporary Church. For the early Christians, the gospel could not be understood apart from that tradition. So it is with us. Reverence for the Church's tradition is what protects us from any sort of chronological or cultural provincialism, such as scholarly fads that arise and carry away a generation of interpreters before being dismissed by the next generation.

The third criterion places scriptural texts within the framework of faith. If we believe that the Scriptures are divinely inspired, we must also believe them to be internally coherent and consistent with all the doctrines that Christians believe. Remember, the Church's dogmas (such as the Real Presence, the papacy, the Immaculate Conception) are not something *added* to Scripture, but are the Church's infallible interpretation *of* Scripture.

Using This Study Guide   This volume is designed to lead the reader through Scripture according to the Church's guidelines—faithful to the canon, to the tradition, and to the creeds. The Church's interpretive principles have thus shaped the component parts of this book, and they are designed to make the reader's study as effective and rewarding as possible.

Introductions: We have introduced the biblical book with an essay covering issues such as authorship, date of composition, purpose, and leading themes. This background information will assist readers to approach and understand the text on its own terms.

Annotations: The basic notes at the bottom of every page help the user to read the Scriptures with understanding. They by no means exhaust the meaning of the sacred text but provide background material to help the reader make sense of what he reads. Often these notes make explicit what the sacred writers assumed or held to be implicit. They also provide scores of historical, cultural, geographical, and theological information pertinent to the inspired narratives—information that can help the reader bridge the distance between the biblical world and his own.

Cross-References: Between the biblical text at the top of each page and the annotations at the bottom, numerous references are listed to point readers to other scriptural passages related to the one being studied. This follow-up is an essential part of any serious study. It is also an excellent way to discover how the content of Scripture "hangs together" in a providential unity. Along with biblical cross-references, the annotations refer to select paragraphs from the *Catechism of the Catholic Church*. These are not doctrinal "proof texts" but are designed to help the reader interpret the Bible in accordance with the mind of the Church. The *Catechism* references listed either handle the biblical text directly or treat a broader doctrinal theme that sheds significant light on that text.

Topical Essays, Word Studies, Charts: These features bring readers to a deeper understanding of select details. The *topical essays* take up major themes and explain them more thoroughly and theologically than the annotations, often relating them to the doctrines of the Church. Occasionally the annotations are supplemented by *word studies* that put readers in touch with the ancient languages of Scripture. These should help readers to understand better and appreciate the inspired terminology that runs throughout the sacred books. Also included are various *charts* that summarize biblical information "at a glance".

Icon Annotations: Three distinctive icons are

interspersed throughout the annotations, each one corresponding to one of the Church's three criteria for biblical interpretation. Bullets indicate the passage or passages to which these icons apply.

Notes marked by the book icon relate to the "content and unity" of Scripture, showing how particular passages of the Old Testament illuminate the mysteries of the New. Much of the information in these notes explains the original context of the citations and indicates how and why this has a direct bearing on Christ or the Church. Through these notes, the reader can develop a sensitivity to the beauty and unity of God's saving plan as it stretches across both Testaments.

Notes marked by the dove icon examine particular passages in light of the Church's "living tradition". Because the Holy Spirit both guides the Magisterium and inspires the spiritual senses of Scripture, these annotations supply information along both of these lines. On the one hand, they refer to the Church's doctrinal teaching as presented by various popes, creeds, and ecumenical councils; on the other, they draw from (and paraphrase) the spiritual interpretations of various Fathers, Doctors, and saints.

Notes marked by the keys icon pertain to the "analogy of faith". Here we spell out how the mysteries of our faith "unlock" and explain one another. This type of comparison between Christian beliefs displays the coherence and unity of defined dogmas, which are the Church's infallible interpretations of Scripture.

Putting It All in Perspective Perhaps the most important context of all we have saved for last: the interior life of the individual reader. What we get out of the Bible will largely depend on how we approach the Bible. Unless we are living a sustained and disciplined life of prayer, we will never have the reverence, the profound humility, or the grace we need to see the Scriptures for what they really are.

You are approaching the "word of God". But for thousands of years, since before he knit you in your mother's womb, the Word of God has been approaching you.

One Final Note. The volume you hold in your hands is only a small part of a much larger work still in production. Study helps similar to those printed in this booklet are being prepared for *all* the books of the Bible and will appear gradually as they are finished. Our ultimate goal is to publish a single, one-volume Study Bible that will include the entire text of Scripture, along with all the annotations, charts, cross-references, maps, and other features found in the following pages. Individual booklets will be published in the meantime, with the hope that God's people can begin to benefit from this labor before its full completion.

We have included a long list of Study Questions in the back to make this format as useful as possible, not only for individual study but for group settings and discussions as well. The questions are designed to help readers both "understand" the Bible and "apply" it to their lives. We pray that God will make use of our efforts and yours to help renew the face of the earth! «

Destinations for the Travels of Saint Paul

INTRODUCTION TO THE
FIRST LETTER OF SAINT PAUL TO THE THESSALONIANS

Author First Thessalonians is a genuine letter of the Apostle Paul. His name opens the epistle (1:1); tradition from earliest times supports this ascription; and only a few modern scholars have ever questioned its authenticity. Indeed, the letter is covered from beginning to end with the unmistakable fingerprints of Paul's language, style, and character known from his other writings. Internal evidence shows us that Paul is writing as the leader and spokesman of his missionary team, which at this time included Silvanus and Timothy (1:1). This explains why so many of his comments and instructions are formulated in the first person plural ("we"/"us"/"our", 1:2; 2:1; 3:1; 4:1; etc).

Date It is widely held that 1 Thessalonians is the oldest letter we have from Paul and may be the oldest book in the entire canon of the NT. By coordinating the report in 3:1–5 with the historical record of Acts 17:1—18:5, most scholars agree that Paul must have penned this letter in the winter months of late A.D. 50 or early 51, soon after Silvanus and Timothy rejoined him in Corinth (Acts 18:5).

Destination Thessalonica was a bustling commercial city founded in 316 B.C. and established by the Romans as the provincial capital of Macedonia (northern Greece) in 146 B.C. The city was ideally situated for trade, having a port into the Aegean Sea and positioned on the Egnatian Way, an overland highway that linked the eastern and western parts of the Mediterranean. Paganism and idolatry dominated the religious environment in Thessalonica, although it was also home to a Jewish colony with at least one synagogue. Paul, Silvanus, and Timothy (1:1) founded the Thessalonian Church in A.D. 50 on the apostle's second missionary tour (Acts 17:1–9). Initially, they spent several weeks preaching in the synagogue and saw the conversion of Jews, Greeks, and several leading women from the city (Acts 17:4). However, enraged by the missionaries' success, certain Jews from the city incited riots and forced the missionaries out of Thessalonica only weeks (or possibly months) after their arrival, causing them trouble as far as Beroea (Acts 17:5, 13). The community left behind remained a target of local persecution (1:6; 2:14; 2 Thess 1:4). A majority of the community were Gentiles who had abandoned idolatry for Christianity (1:9).

Purpose and Themes First Thessalonians is a predominantly pastoral letter with a pastoral focus. Paul wrote out of a deep concern for these recent converts who were unexpectedly left alone to withstand the rising tide of persecution and the constant pressures of paganism. Absent in person and eager to return (3:10), Paul sent the epistle in his place to strengthen them through these difficult times (3:3–5), to encourage them to be chaste and charitable (4:1–12), and to console the bereaved among them with the hope of resurrection (4:13–14). Expressions of joy, gratitude, and encouragement punctuate the letter as Paul affirms them for their astonishing growth (1:8) in faith, hope, and love (1:3; 3:6; 5:8). There are no rebukes for the Thessalonians, only appeals to stay on the same course (4:1; 5:11).

The substance of the letter, though more personal than theological, is not lacking in doctrinal content. This is evident in Paul's emphasis on eschatology (teaching concerning the end times). At least once in every chapter he mentions the return of Jesus Christ in glory. According to Paul, Christ will come again from heaven to deliver us "from the wrath to come" (1:10) and give us the final "salvation" for which we yearn (5:9). His prayer is that Christ will perfect the "love" of his readers (3:12) and establish them forever in "holiness" at his arrival (3:13; 5:23). The apostle is confident he will be proud of the Thessalonians on that day and expects to wear them like a "crown" before the Lord (2:19). The subject of eschatology has pressing importance for certain readers who are anxious about the fate of their deceased relatives and friends (4:13). Paul assures them that, as God raised Jesus from the dead and carried him into heaven, so too he will raise the righteous at the blast of the final trumpet and escort them into glory (4:14–18). Because the last day will "come like a thief" (5:2), Paul challenges readers to stay awake both morally and spiritually in anticipation of the Second Coming (5:1–11). Otherwise they will be caught unprepared when Jesus returns as Judge to avenge the wicked for their evil deeds (4:6). In Paul's mind, this itinerary for the end of days is revealed to give comfort and hope to the saints struggling on earth (4:18).

OUTLINE OF THE FIRST LETTER OF SAINT PAUL TO THE THESSALONIANS

1. **Opening Address (1:1)**

2. **Memories of the Past (1:2—3:13)**
   A. Thanksgiving (1:2–10)
   B. Paul's Thessalonian Ministry (2:1–16)
   C. The Mission and Report of Timothy (2:17—3:10)
   D. Prayer for Sanctification (3:11–13)

3. **Instructions for the Future (4:1—5:22)**
   A. An Appeal for Purity (4:1–8)
   B. An Appeal for Love and Labor (4:9–12)
   C. The Return of Jesus (4:13–18)
   D. The Day of the Lord (5:1–11)
   E. Final Exhortations (5:12–22)

4. **Conclusion (5:23–28)**

THE FIRST LETTER OF SAINT PAUL TO THE
THESSALONIANS

Salutation

1 Paul, Silva'nus, and Timothy,
To the Church of the Thessalo'nians in God the Father and the Lord Jesus Christ:
Grace to you and peace.

The Thessalonians' Faith and Example

2 We give thanks to God always for you all, constantly mentioning you in our prayers, ³remembering before our God and Father your work of faith and labor of love and steadfastness of hope in our Lord Jesus Christ. ⁴For we know, brethren beloved by God, that he has chosen you; ⁵for our gospel came to you not only in word, but also in power and in the Holy Spirit and with full conviction. You know what kind of men we proved to be among you for your sake. ⁶And you became imitators of us and of the Lord, for you received the word in much affliction, with joy inspired by the Holy Spirit; ⁷so that you became an example to all the believers in Macedonia and in Acha'ia. ⁸For not only has the word of the Lord sounded forth from you in Macedonia and Acha'ia, but your faith in God has gone forth everywhere, so that we need not say anything. ⁹For they themselves report concerning us what a welcome we had among you, and how you turned to God from idols, to serve a living and true God, ¹⁰and to wait for his Son from heaven, whom he raised from the dead, Jesus who delivers us from the wrath to come.

1:1: 2 Thess 1:1; 2 Cor 1:19; Acts 16:1; 17:1; Rom 1:7. **1:2:** 2 Thess 1:3; 2:13; Rom 1:9.
1:3: 2 Thess 1:11; 1:3; Rom 8:25; 15:4; Gal 1:4. **1:4:** 2 Thess 2:13; Rom 1:7; 2 Pet 1:10. **1:5:** 2 Thess 2:14; Rom 15:19.
1:6: Col 2:2; 1 Thess 2:10; 1 Cor 4:16; 11:1; Acts 17:5–10; 13:52. **1:7:** Rom 15:26; Acts 18:12.
1:8: 2 Thess 3:1; Rom 1:8. **1:10:** Mt 3:7.

1:1 Paul: The author of the letter (2:18) as well as the founding apostle of the Thessalonian Church (Acts 17:1–9). **Silvanus:** A Latin transcription of the name "Silas", a Christian prophet from Jerusalem (Acts 15:32) who accompanied Paul on his second missionary journey (Acts 15:40). He was a co-founder with Paul of the church in Thessalonica. **Timothy:** A young man selected by Paul to minister with him and Silas on their missionary adventures (Acts 16:1–4). Without stating it explicitly, Acts implies that Timothy played a secondary role with Paul and Silas in evangelizing Thessalonica (Acts 17:1, 14). He was later sent to encourage the community and report back to Paul on their situation (3:1–6). See note on 1 Tim 1:2. **in . . . the Father and the Lord:** The Church family in Thessalonica is united "in" the divine family of the Trinity. The heavenly Father has made this possible by choosing believers for adoption (1:4), giving them the Holy Spirit (4:8), and promising to raise even their bodies from the dead (4:14) when his Son returns in glory (1:10; 4:15–17) (CCC 2014). **Grace to you and peace:** A standard Christian greeting used by Paul and other writers in the NT (1 Pet 1:2; 2 Jn 3; Rev 1:4).

1:2 We give thanks: Nearly every Pauline epistle opens with expressions of gratitude (Rom 1:8; 1 Cor 1:4; etc.). Paul is particularly thankful for the Thessalonians, who have admirably committed themselves to living out the gospel (1:8; 3:6; 4:1, 10).

1:3 remembering: Paul recalls the time he first spent with his readers. What stands out in his mind are the theological virtues that changed their lives: in **faith** they abandoned their idols and embraced the living God (1:9); in **hope** they endured suffering and expressed longing for the final salvation that Jesus will bring when he returns (1:10; 5:9); and in **love** they served one another in generous and sacrificial ways (4:9–10). These virtues will protect them like armor in the challenging days ahead (5:8). Paul often reflects on this triad of Christian virtues

in his writings (Rom 5:1–5; 1 Cor 13:8–13; Gal 5:5–6; Col 1:4–5) (CCC 1812–29). See note on 1 Cor 13:13.

1:4 he has chosen you: Before the founding of the world, the Father chose believers for salvation (5:9) and divine sonship (Eph 1:4–5) (CCC 759). See note on Rom 8:29.

1:5 also in power: The power of God bursts forth through the gospel to save sinners who accept it with faith (Rom 1:16). It is also possible that Paul is referring to the powerful signs and miracles that accompanied his preaching and gave incentive for faith (2 Cor 12:12; Gal 3:5).

1:6 affliction, with joy: Suffering for the gospel is a sign of blessedness and divine approval (Mt 5:10; 1 Pet 3:14). It makes the believer more like Christ (1 Pet 2:21) and his apostles (3:3–4).

1:7 Macedonia . . . Achaia: Two Roman provinces that correspond to northern and southern Greece. Paul is writing from the Achaian city of Corinth in the south, while his readers are residents of the Macedonian city of Thessalonica in the north.

1:9 turned to God from idols: Suggests most of the Thessalonians were Gentile converts, although some Jewish converts were made in the local synagogue (Acts 17:4).
● Paul is voicing a traditional Jewish critique of idolatry. In the Scriptures, Yahweh is acknowledged and praised as the only *living* God in contrast to the *lifeless* idols of the pagans (Tob 14:6; Ps 135:13–18; Jer 10:6–10; Hab 2:18–20). Regarding belief in the one true God, the faith of Israel (Deut 6:4) remains the faith of the Church (1 Cor 8:6). This was the cutting edge of Paul's preaching among Gentile audiences immersed in polytheistic cultures (Acts 14:15; 17:22–31) (CCC 212).

1:10 his Son from heaven: The first of several references in the letter to the return of Jesus (2:19; 3:13; 4:16; 5:23). See note on 1 Thess 4:13–18. **the wrath to come:** The final unleashing of God's power against evil on Judgment Day (Rom 2:8). The faithful in Christ will be spared the condemnation and

Paul's Ministry in Thessalonica

2 For you yourselves know, brethren, that our visit to you was not in vain; [2]but though we had already suffered and been shamefully treated at Philip′pi, as you know, we had courage in our God to declare to you the gospel of God in the face of great opposition. [3]For our appeal does not spring from error or uncleanness, nor is it made with guile; [4]but just as we have been approved by God to be entrusted with the gospel, so we speak, not to please men, but to please God who tests our hearts. [5]For we never used either words of flattery, as you know, or a cloak for greed, as God is witness; [6]nor did we seek glory from men, whether from you or from others, though we might have made demands as apostles of Christ. [7]But we were gentle [a] among you, like a nurse taking care of her children. [8]So, being affectionately desirous of you, we were ready to share with you not only the gospel of God but also our own selves, because you had become very dear to us.

9 For you remember our labor and toil, brethren; we worked night and day, that we might not burden any of you, while we preached to you the gospel of God. [10]You are witnesses, and God also, how holy and righteous and blameless was our behavior to you believers; [11]for you know how, like a father with his children, we exhorted each one of you and encouraged you and charged you [12]to walk in a manner worthy of God, who calls you into his own kingdom and glory.

13 And we also thank God constantly for this, that when you received the word of God which you heard from us, you accepted it not as the word of men but as what it really is, the word of God, which is at work in you believers. [14]For you, brethren, became imitators of the churches of God in Christ Jesus which are in Judea; for you suffered the same things from your own countrymen as they did from the Jews, [15]who killed both the Lord Jesus and the prophets, and drove us out, and displease God and oppose all men [16]by hindering us

---

2:2: Acts 16:19–24; 17:1–9; Rom 1:1.   **2:5:** Acts 20:33.   **2:6:** 1 Cor 9:1.   **2:7:** 1 Thess 2:11; Gal 4:19.
2:8: 2 Cor 12:15; 1 Jn 3:16.   **2:11:** 1 Cor4:14.   **2:12:** 1 Pet 5:10.   **2:13:** 1 Thess 1:2.
2:14: 1 Thess 1:6; 1 Cor 7:17; Gal 1:22; Acts 17:5; 2 Thess 1:4.   **2:15:** Lk 24:20; Acts 2:23; 7:52.
2:16: Acts 9:23; 13:45, 50; 14:2, 5, 19; 17:5, 13; 18:12; 21:21, 27; 25:2, 7; 1 Cor 10:33; Gen 15:16; 1 Thess 1:10.

---

everlasting destruction in store for the wicked (2 Thess 1:7–10) (CCC 681).

2:2 shamefully treated at Philippi: Just before coming to Thessalonica, Paul and Silas were hauled before the city magistrates of Philippi, stripped of their clothes, beaten with rods, and thrown into prison (Acts 16:19–24). This might have disheartened or terrified them into silence, but God gave them the **courage** to keep moving and preaching despite aggressive opposition (Rom 1:16).

2:3 error . . . uncleanness . . . guile: Perhaps Paul, in defending his motives, is countering slanderous charges circulated by his enemies. Despite such calumnies, his missionary team at all times lived and worked above reproach (2:10).

2:6 apostles: Refers to Paul, Silvanus, and Timothy (1:1). In the NT, the term "apostle" is used in several different ways. It can refer to (1) Jesus, the One sent by the Father (Heb 3:1), (2) the twelve disciples chosen by Jesus (Lk 6:13), (3) a group of witnesses to the Resurrection (1 Cor 15:7), and (4) messengers sent on missions by churches (2 Cor 8:23; Phil 2:25).

2:7 like a nurse: Or, "like a nursing mother". The idea is that Paul and his companions developed a tender affection for the Thessalonians and made every effort to encourage them and serve their needs (2:8).

2:9 labor and toil: As apostles, Paul and his coworkers are entitled to financial and material support from the communities under their care (Lk 10:7; 1 Cor 9:13–14). But during their brief stay with the Thessalonians, they waived this right to avoid loading the Church down with burdens and to show that their ministry was not driven by greed or self-interest. It is not specified how the missionaries supported themselves, but we know that Paul was a tentmaker by trade (Acts 18:3). **night and day:** Accentuates how tirelessly the apostles worked in order to provide for themselves and to continue their ministry at the same time. Paul, for one, was glad to spend himself in this way (2 Cor 12:15).

2:11 like a father: With great fatherly care, Paul has overseen the moral and spiritual formation of his Thessalonian children begotten through the gospel. The comparisons used here and in 2:7 highlight both the maternal and paternal sides of Paul's ministry. See note on 1 Cor 4:15.

2:12 God, who calls you: The Father summons his children to a royal inheritance kept in heaven (1 Pet 1:14). The saints will be given the fullness of this heavenly kingdom, but those unworthy of the calling will be denied it (1 Cor 6:9–10; Eph 5:5).

2:13 the word of God: The revealed gospel (1 Pet 1:25). This saving message was written down in the books of the NT and delivered orally in the form of apostolic preaching (2 Thess 2:15; CCC 104, 1349). ● The ministry of the apostles parallels the ministry of the Hebrew Prophets, who received the word of the Lord and announced it to Israel by word of mouth and in writing (1 Kings 17:1–2; Jer 1:4; Ezek 1:3; Hos 1:1).

2:14–16 Paul has some unusually harsh words for the perpetrators of Christian persecution. He traces this madness back to Jerusalem, whose long history of mistreating the Prophets (Mt 23:37) reached a new and diabolical level when its leaders murdered Jesus the Messiah (2:15; Acts 2:23). The Thessalonians got a taste of this when Jewish zealots, fiercely loyal to the aims and outlook of Judean Judaism, stirred up a horde of angry locals to raid the house church where Paul and his companions were staying (Acts 17:5–9). Similar forms of harassment continued even after the missionaries fled (3:3; 2 Thess 1:5). Notice that Paul is criticizing Jewish persecutors, not the Jewish people in general. Years later Paul still insisted that Jews have first claim to the gospel (Rom 1:16), and he expected that "all Israel" would be saved (Rom 11:26) (CCC 597). See essay: *The Salvation of All Israel* at Rom 11.

2:14 in Judea: Attacks on the infant Church began with the martyrdom of Stephen in Jerusalem (Acts 7:58–8:1). Even Paul, by his own admission, was a persecutor of Christians before his conversion (Gal 1:22–23; 1 Cor 15:9). **your own countrymen:** Macedonian pagans, but also hostile opponents from the Thessalonian synagogue (Acts 17:5). **the Jews:** I.e., the Palestinian Jews responsible for terrorizing Judean churches.

2:16 fill up the measure: Paul imagines a cup that is full of iniquity and is about to brim over. Jesus used the same image

---

[a] Other ancient authorities read *babes*.

from speaking to the Gentiles that they may be saved—so as always to fill up the measure of their sins. But God's wrath has come upon them at last! [b]

Paul's Desire to Visit the Thessalonians Again

17 But since we were deprived of you, brethren, for a short time, in person not in heart, we endeavored the more eagerly and with great desire to see you face to face; [18]because we wanted to come to you—I, Paul, again and again—but Satan hindered us. [19]For what is our hope or joy or crown of boasting before our Lord Jesus at his coming? Is it not you? [20]For you are our glory and joy.

3 Therefore when we could bear it no longer, we were willing to be left behind at Athens alone, [2]and we sent Timothy, our brother and God's servant in the gospel of Christ, to establish you in your faith and to exhort you, [3]that no one be moved by these afflictions. You yourselves know that this is to be our lot. [4]For when we were with you, we told you beforehand that we were to suffer affliction; just as it has come to pass, and as you know. [5]For this reason, when I could bear it no longer, I sent that I might know your faith, for fear that somehow the tempter had tempted you and that our labor would be in vain.

Timothy's Good Report

6 But now that Timothy has come to us from you, and has brought us the good news of your faith and love and reported that you always remember us kindly and long to see us, as we long to see you—[7]for this reason, brethren, in all our distress and affliction we have been comforted about you through your faith; [8]for now we live, if you stand fast in the Lord. [9]For what thanksgiving can we render to God for you, for all the joy which we feel for your sake before our God, [10]praying earnestly night and day that we may see you face to face and supply what is lacking in your faith?

2:17: 1 Cor 5:3.   2:19: Phil 4:1; 1 Thess 3:13; 4:15; 5:23; Mt 16:27; Mk 8:38.   2:20: 2 Cor 1:14.
3:1: Phil 2:19; Acts 17:15.   3:2: 2 Cor 1:1; Col 1:1.   3:3: Acts 14:22.   3:4: 1 Thess2:14.
3:5: Mt 4:3; Phil 2:16.   3:6: Acts 18:5.

---

against the Pharisees when he prophesied the destruction of Jerusalem within the first Christian generation (Mt 23:32). **wrath has come upon them:** Perhaps in the form of divine abandonment of the people to sin (Rom 1:18, 24, 26, 28), which is an ominous prelude to the final manifestation of divine wrath in A.D. 70 with the downfall of Jerusalem, the destruction of the Temple, and the dispersion of unbelieving Israel (Lk 21:23). A nearly identical statement appears in Jewish tra-

[b] Or *completely*, or *for ever*.

Word Study

At Last (1 Thess 2:16)

Eis telos (Gk.): a phrase that can mean "finally", "until the end", or "to the utmost". It is used six times in the NT, usually in the Gospels. In Matthew and Mark, Jesus says that the believer who keeps the faith and endures "to the end" will be saved (Mt 10:22; 24:13; Mk 13:13). In Luke, Jesus describes an oppressed widow who will "finally" or "eventually" wear out an unrighteous judge by her continual pleas for justice (Lk 18:5). In John, Jesus assures the disciples he has loved them "to the fullest extent" (Jn 13:1). Paul's intention in using the expression in 1 Thess 2:16 is a matter of interpretation. (1) It could mean "to the utmost degree" and describe how the full retribution of heaven is coming upon unbelieving Jews in Judea. (2) It could also mean "finally" and express how the wrath they have coming to them has at long last arrived. (3) Finally, it could mean "to the end" and describe how divine wrath will press upon unbelieving Jews for the rest of history. Deciding among these options is difficult, though one of the first two possibilities makes the most sense of the passage within its context.

dition that describes the violent conquest of the city of Shechem (*Testament of Levi* 6, 11). For Paul, the wrath poured out on Jewish persecutors prefigures the "wrath to come" upon sinners at the final return of Jesus (1:10; 2 Thess 1:7–9).

2:17 deprived: The Greek can mean "orphaned", a reference to Paul's hurried departure from Thessalonica (Acts 17:10).

2:18 Satan hindered us: The nature of the obstruction is left unspecified. It may be linked with the Jewish and pagan opposition Paul faced in Thessalonica (Acts 17:5). Now, the same evil that forced him to flee also prevents him from returning.

2:19 crown of boasting: The expression Paul uses is found in the Greek OT at Prov 16:31 and Ezek 16:12. Here it signifies the pride that Paul will take in his readers when the day of rewards has come. **his coming:** Several times the word "coming" (Gk. *parousia*) is used in the Thessalonian letters for the anticipated return of Christ in glory (3:13; 4:15; 5:23; 2 Thess 2:1, 8). For some of its background and meaning, see word study: *Coming* at Mt 24:3.

2:20 our glory and joy: Paul had similar sentiments for the Philippian Church (Phil 4:1).

3:1 at Athens: According to Acts 17:10–15, Paul and his missionary team escaped Thessalonica by night, traveled overland to Beroea, and then Paul went on by himself to Athens. Apparently Silas and Timothy rejoined him in Athens shortly thereafter.

3:2 we sent Timothy: Restless and anxious for the welfare of the Thessalonians, Paul and Silas sent Timothy on a mission to encourage and reassure the recently abandoned community. He returned after Paul had left Athens for Corinth (Acts 18:5). He brought a glowing report of how fast the believers were growing in virtue and how deeply they longed to see Paul again (3:6). This heartening news was a comfort to the suffering apostle (3:7).

3:3 these afflictions: Tribulation and distress are the inevitable lot of the true apostle (1 Cor 4:9–13). In this way, Jesus reproduces his own experience of suffering in the lives of his ordained shepherds (2 Cor 4:8–12). The Thessalonians are also sharing in these afflictions (2:14).

3:10 what is lacking: Gaps remain in the catechetical instruction of the Thessalonians. Paul hopes to fill these gaps by returning to complete the process of Christian formation in person (3:11).

11 Now may our God and Father himself, and our Lord Jesus, direct our way to you; ^{12}and may the Lord make you increase and abound in love to one another and to all men, as we do to you, ^{13}so that he may establish your hearts unblamable in holiness before our God and Father, at the coming of our Lord Jesus with all his saints.

A Life Pleasing to God

4 Finally, brethren, we beg and exhort you in the Lord Jesus, that as you learned from us how you ought to walk and to please God, just as you are doing, you do so more and more. ^{2}For you know what instructions we gave you through the Lord Jesus. ^{3}For this is the will of God, your sanctification: that you abstain from immorality; ^{4}that each one of you know how to control his own body in holiness and honor, ^{5}not in the passion of lust like heathens who do not know God; ^{6}that no man transgress, and wrong his brother in this

matter, ^{c} because the Lord is an avenger in all these things, as we solemnly forewarned you. ^{7}For God has not called us for uncleanness, but in holiness. ^{8}Therefore whoever disregards this, disregards not man but God, who gives his Holy Spirit to you.

9 But concerning love of the brethren you have no need to have any one write to you, for you yourselves have been taught by God to love one another; ^{10}and indeed you do love all the brethren throughout Macedonia. But we exhort you, brethren, to do so more and more, ^{11}to aspire to live quietly, to mind your own affairs, and to work with your hands, as we charged you; ^{12}so that you may command the respect of outsiders, and be dependent on nobody.

The Coming of the Lord

13 But we would not have you ignorant, brethren, concerning those who are asleep, that you may not grieve as others do who have no hope.

3:13: 1 Cor 1:8; 1 Thess 2:19; 4:17. **4:3:** 1 Cor 6:18. **4:4:** 1 Cor 7:2; 1 Pet 3:7.
4:11: 2 Thess 3:12; Eph 4:28; 2 Thess 3:10–12. **4:13:** Eph 2:12.

3:12 abound in love: I.e., in the divine love that Christ pours into our hearts through the Spirit (Rom 5:5). It reaches out to **one another** in the family of faith as well as to **all** persons in the family of man, friends and enemies alike (Mt 5:43–48). Because the Lord is the Giver of this gift, only he can make it increase and overflow (CCC 1825).

3:13 holiness: Moral and spiritual sanctity. See note on 1 Thess 4:3. **the coming:** The third mention of Christ's return so far in the letter (1:10; 2:19). See note on 1 Thess 2:19. **all his saints:** Or, "all his holy ones". This could refer to the blessed angels or the victorious saints or both. Most likely, Paul is saying that Christ will descend from heaven with an army of holy angels. This is the picture drawn by Jesus (Mk 8:38), by the OT (Zech 14:5), and by Paul himself in his follow-up letter (2 Thess 1:7).

4:1–5:22 The second half of the letter turns from memories of the past to moral exhortations for the days ahead. Paul is pleased with the moral progress being made in Thessalonica and urges them to grow still more (4:1; 5:11).

4:3 sanctification: Holiness of life is willed by God. Growth in holiness, or progressive sanctification, is a process that begins with God's work in Baptism (1 Cor 6:11) and continues when believers abound in love (3:12–13) and exert the moral effort needed to overcome sinful and selfish habits (Rom 6:19). Paul here demands the sanctification of the body through chastity, though the ultimate goal is a complete sanctification of the person (5:23). Holiness is not optional for believers but is a condition for salvation (Heb 12:14) (CCC 2348–50, 2813). • Vatican II issued a universal call to holiness for clergy and laity alike that is expressed through the perfection of love (*Lumen Gentium* 39). **abstain from immorality:** Specifically, from the various forms of sexual immorality widely accepted in pagan environments such as Thessalonica. The Greek expression used here is also found in the apostolic decree issued by the Jerusalem Council in A.D. 49 (Acts 15:20, 29). Paul, Silas, and Timothy (1:1) went about delivering this decree on the second missionary tour in Acts (Acts 16:4). See note on Acts 15:20.

4:4 his own body: Literally, "his own vessel". Both ancient and modern interpreters are divided over the precise meaning of the term "vessel", which could refer to one's *body* (2 Cor 4:7) or one's *wife* (1 Pet 3:7). If the former, Paul is advocating

chastity and self-control in contrast to the lust of the pagans (Tertullian, St. John Chrysostom); if the latter, Paul is advocating the honorable pursuit of marriage, not as an outlet for lust, but as a pure and holy partnership in the Lord (St. Augustine, St. Thomas Aquinas). Either way, Paul is urging readers to master the passions associated with human sexuality.

4:5 do not know God: Pagans live in darkness and ignorance until the gospel enlightens their way (Ps 78:6; Jer 10:25; Gal 4:8).

4:6 wrong his brother: The context suggests Paul is thinking of adultery, a form of bodily "uncleanness" (4:7). Not only are the involved partners defiled by this impurity, but they wrong their spouses and bring shame on their families as well (CCC 2380–81).

4:8 his Holy Spirit: Unchastity is an outrage against God, whose presence dwells in our bodies and makes them temples of holiness (1 Cor 6:18–20; CCC 2351–56).

4:9 love of the brethren: Fraternal love for brothers and sisters in the faith is the mark of a true disciple of Christ (Jn 13:35). The Thessalonians are learning this lesson well as their charity is spreading throughout the province of Macedonia (1 Thess 4:10). See note on 1 Thess 3:12.

4:11 mind your own affairs: A humble and quiet life is all the more necessary in Thessalonica, where disciples are living under clouds of suspicion and distrust (Acts 17:5–9). **work with your hands:** Paul frowns upon idleness (5:14). Believers must be dependable and hard-working people who labor for the Lord and not just their employers (Col 3:23). This not only leads to personal sanctification, but it will earn the respect of coworkers and neighbors as well (CCC 2427).

4:13–18 Paul comforts the bereaved with the hope of resurrection. Apparently some were concerned that the faithful departed would be left behind when Jesus returns to bring the saints to heaven. Paul insists otherwise: the righteous dead will be raised in glory and gathered to Christ even before the generation of believers still living on the earth in the last days.

4:13 asleep: A metaphor for death. In Scripture, the expression hints that death is only a temporary state that will end when the righteous are awakened at the resurrection (Is 26:19; Dan 12:2). The gospel tells us that death is not extinction or the end of all things, but a step closer to eternal life (CCC 1010, 1016). For the state of the soul after bodily death, see note on 2 Cor 5:8. **may not grieve:** It is human to mourn the death of a loved one; it is Christian to keep our sadness from

---

^{c} Or *defraud his brother in business.*

¹⁴For since we believe that Jesus died and rose again, even so, through Jesus, God will bring with him those who have fallen asleep. ¹⁵For this we declare to you by the word of the Lord, that we who are alive, who are left until the coming of the Lord, shall not precede those who have fallen asleep. ¹⁶For the Lord himself will descend from heaven with a cry of command, with the archangel's call, and with the sound of the trumpet of God. And the dead in Christ will rise first; ¹⁷then we who are alive, who are left, shall be caught up together with them in the clouds to meet the Lord in the air; and so we shall always be with the Lord. ¹⁸Therefore comfort one another with these words.

5 But as to the times and the seasons, brethren, you have no need to have anything written to you. ²For you yourselves know well that the day of the Lord will come like a thief in the night. ³When people say, "There is peace and security," then sudden destruction will come upon them as labor pains come upon a woman with child, and there will be no escape. ⁴But you are not in darkness, brethren, for that day to surprise you like a thief. ⁵For you are all sons of light and sons of the day; we are not of the night or of darkness. ⁶So then let us not sleep, as others do, but let us keep awake and be sober. ⁷For those who sleep sleep at night, and those who get drunk are drunk at night. ⁸But, since we belong to the day, let us be sober, and put on the breastplate of faith and love, and for a helmet the hope of salvation. ⁹For God has not destined us for wrath, but to obtain salvation through our Lord

---

4:14: 2 Cor 4:14.   **4:16:** Mt 24:31; 1 Cor 15:23; 2 Thess 2:1.   **5:1:** Acts 1:7.   **5:2:** 1 Cor 1:8.   **5:3:** 2 Thess 1:9.
5:4: 1 Jn 2:8; Acts 26:18.   **5:5:** Lk 16:8.   **5:6:** Rom 13:11; 1 Pet 1:13.   **5:7:** Acts 2:15; 2 Pet 2:13.
5:8: Eph 6:14, 23, 17; Rom 8:24.   **5:9:** 1 Thess 1:10; 2 Thess 2:13; Rom 14:9.

---

sliding down to despair. Every sorrow in life can be softened by the joyful hope that the dead will live again when Jesus returns (CCC 1001).

✠ **4:14 Jesus died and rose again:** The guarantee of our own bodily resurrection (Rom 8:11; CCC 989). See note on Lk 24:39. ● Christ is the pattern of our resurrection because he assumed flesh and rose again embodied in flesh. He is also the cause of our resurrection, for what was done by Christ's humanity was done, not only by the power of his human nature, but also in virtue of his divinity. It was not merely his body that rose, but a body united to the Word of life (St. Thomas Aquinas, *Commentary on 1 Thessalonians* 4, 2).

4:15 we who are alive: In contrast to "those who are asleep" (4:13). The distinction is between living and deceased Christians and the order in which they will ascend to meet Christ at his coming. Some infer from Paul's use of "we" that the apostle believed Christ would come again soon, perhaps within his own lifetime. If Paul cherished such a hope, the text does not assert this explicitly. Paul professes to know nothing precise about the timing of the Lord's return beyond its suddenness (5:1-2). Other passages indicate that Paul envisioned death as a real possibility for himself (Phil 3:10-11; 2 Tim 4:6) and numbered himself among those who would be raised from the dead (1 Cor 6:14; 2 Cor 4:14). See note on 1 Cor 15:51.

📖 **4:16-17** Paul depicts the coming of Jesus with apocalyptic imagery that was widely used in Jewish literature from this period. ● Several dramatic scenes in the Bible also use this imagery and prepare the way for this final event of history. **(1)** During the Exodus, the Lord *descended* upon Sinai with a fiery *cloud* and a blaring *trumpet*, and all Israel went forth to *meet* him (Ex 19:16-20). **(2)** During the Conquest, Israel joined forces with the *angels* of the Lord to bring down the walls of Jericho with a blast of seven *trumpets* and a loud *cry* from the people (Josh 5:13-14; 6:15-20). **(3)** In the visions of Daniel, a court sits in *judgment* as it watches the Messiah riding the *clouds* into heaven and receiving from God an eternal *kingdom* that he shares with the saints (Dan 7:10-14, 18, 27).

4:16 the Lord himself: Christ will descend to earth "in the same way" that he ascended into heaven, i.e., enveloped in a glorious cloud (Acts 1:11). **cry of command:** The voice of the Son of man that calls forth the dead from their tombs and summons them to the judgment (Jn 5:28-29). **archangel's call:** Possibly the voice of Michael, the guardian of the people of God (Dan 12:1) and the leader of the angelic army (Jude 9; Rev 12:7). **the trumpet:** The final blast that inaugurates the resurrection and glorification of the saints. For its biblical background, see note on 1 Cor 15:52. **the dead in Christ:** The faithful departed, though temporarily deprived of their bodies,

live on in spiritual union with the Lord as they await the resurrection (2 Cor 5:8).

4:17 caught up: Or, "raptured". Believers living on the earth when Christ returns will be drawn up to join the saints of the ages as they ascend into glory. Paul seems to assert, not that the final generation will die and then be raised, but that their bodies will be instantly glorified and made immortal. This is how Paul was understood by the Greek Fathers of the Church, and this agrees with the prophetic outlook of 1 Cor 15:51-53.

5:1-11 Continuing his reflections on the Second Coming, Paul adds a warning that believers must be watchful and ready. Christ will return unexpectedly, so unless we live in the light and arm ourselves with divine virtues (5:8), we will be taken by surprise and delivered to sudden destruction (5:3). His words discourage attempts to speculate about the precise timing of Christ's return (CCC 672-73, 2849).

📖 **5:1 the times and the seasons:** An expression used elsewhere in Acts 1:7 in the NT and Dan 2:21 in the OT. In both contexts, it refers to predetermined dates when God establishes kingdoms.

5:2 day of the Lord: The appointed day when Christ the Lord will come again as Savior (Heb 9:28) and Judge (Mt 25:31-46). Paul does not know when this day will arrive; he knows only some of the signs that will lead up to it (2 Thess 2:1-12). Liturgically, this final and fateful day is anticipated every Lord's day, when believers gather for eucharistic worship (Rev 1:10) and receive either blessings or curses at Christ's table (Jn 6:54; 1 Cor 11:27-32). Historically, it is prefigured by the return of Jesus to judge Israel and Jerusalem in A.D. 70. **like a thief:** I.e., suddenly and unexpectedly (Mt 24:43-44; Rev 3:3).

5:3 peace and security: The slogan of the foolish and unprepared (Jer 6:14). **destruction:** Not annihilation or extinction, but eternal separation from God (2 Thess 1:9). **labor pains:** The wicked will be seized with sudden contractions of pain that will intensify and never subside (Hos 13:12-13).

5:5 sons of light: A Semitic way of saying "sons of goodness, righteousness, and truth" (Eph 5:8-9). The struggle between light and darkness as forces of good and evil is a prominent theme in Jewish tradition (Dead Sea Scrolls) and the NT (Jn 1:4-9; Acts 26:18; Rom 13:12-13; 1 Jn 1:5-7) (CCC 1216).

5:8 breastplate . . . helmet: The virtues of faith, hope, and love are the defensive gear of the believer, protecting the head and heart during the battles of life. These conflicts are engaged not only with the passions and enticements of the world, but also with demonic spirits that seek our demise (Eph 6:13-17). Paul often reminds readers of their spiritual armory in Christ (Rom 13:12; 2 Cor 6:7; 10:3-4). See note on 1 Thess 1:3.

Jesus Christ, [10]who died for us so that whether we wake or sleep we might live with him. [11]Therefore encourage one another and build one another up, just as you are doing.

Final Exhortations, Greetings, and Benediction

12 But we beg you, brethren, to respect those who labor among you and are over you in the Lord and admonish you, [13]and to esteem them very highly in love because of their work. Be at peace among yourselves. [c2] [14]And we exhort you, brethren, admonish the idle, encourage the faint-hearted, help the weak, be patient with them all. [15]See that none of you repays evil for evil, but always seek to do good to one another and to all. [16]Rejoice always, [17]pray constantly, [18]give thanks in all circumstances; for this is the will of God in Christ Jesus for you. [19]Do not quench the Spirit, [20]do not despise prophesying, [21]but test everything; hold fast what is good, [22]abstain from every form of evil.

23 May the God of peace himself sanctify you wholly; and may your spirit and soul and body be kept sound and blameless at the coming of our Lord Jesus Christ. [24]He who calls you is faithful, and he will do it.

25 Brethren, pray for us.

26 Greet all the brethren with a holy kiss.

27 I adjure you by the Lord that this letter be read to all the brethren.

28 The grace of our Lord Jesus Christ be with you.

5:12: 1 Cor 16:18; 1 Tim 5:17; 1 Cor 16:16; Rom 16:6, 12; 1 Cor 15:10; Heb 13:17.   **5:13:** Mk 9:50.
5:14: Is 35:4; Rom 14:1; 1 Cor 8:7; 2 Thess 3:6, 7, 11.   **5:15:** Rom 12:17; 1 Pet 3:9.   **5:16:** Phil 4:4.   **5:17:** Eph 6:18
5:18: Eph 5:20.   **5:19:** Eph 4:30.   **5:20:** 1 Cor 14:31.   **5:21:** 1 Cor 14:29; 1 Jn 4:1.   **5:23:** Rom 15:33.
5:26: Rom 16:16.   **5:27:** Col 4:16.   **5:28:** Rom 16:20; 2 Thess 3:18.

5:10 who died for us: Even in a letter dominated by the hope of Christ's return, Paul never loses sight of Christ's redemptive death.

5:12 over you in the Lord: A hierarchical ministry of leadership was already in place in Thessalonica. This is not surprising, since it was Paul's policy to ordain presbyters (priests) to shepherd the flock in his missionary churches (Acts 14:23; Tit 1:5). The spiritual oversight of these pastors entitles them to the respect and submission of the laity (CCC 1269).
• Love priests as children love their fathers. Through them you have received an eternal generation, you have obtained the kingdom, and the gates of heaven are swung open to you. If you love Christ and the kingdom of heaven, then acknowledge through whom you obtained it (St. John Chrysostom, *Homilies on 1 Thessalonians* 10).

5:14 admonish the idle: Paul has no sympathy for freeloaders who expect to eat but are unwilling to work. This is an embarrassing problem in Thessalonica and needs to be addressed firmly by the congregation (2 Thess 3:6–13). See note on 1 Thess 4:11.

5:15 evil for evil: The gospel forbids personal retaliation (Mt 5:38–42; Rom 12:17–19).

5:17 pray constantly: I.e., pray regularly, but we should also allow the spirit of prayer and praise to envelop our work and daily activities (Eph 6:18). Whatever we do can be done for the greater glory of God (Col 3:17) (CCC 1174, 2743).

5:19 Do not quench the Spirit: I.e., by resisting the movement of the Spirit and the exercise of his gifts (1 Cor 12:4–11). Paul's only proviso is that they test prophesies and alleged revelations to make sure they line up with the truths of the gospel (Rom 12:6; 1 Cor 14:29) (CCC 696, 799–801).
• When a person is moved by the Spirit to do something generous, and someone else impedes him, the one who impedes quenches the Spirit. Also, when someone commits mortal sin, the Spirit ceases to abide in him. A third way to quench the Spirit is to conceal our gifts instead of using them for the benefit of others (St. Thomas Aquinas, *Commentary on 1 Thessalonians* 5).

5:23 spirit and soul and body: Paul is emphasizing the wholeness of the person without intending to make precise distinctions between his component parts. A certain distinction can be made, however, if we understand the *body* as the material frame, the *soul* as its immaterial principle of life, and the *spirit* as the human capacity for prayer and worship (Rom 1:9; 1 Cor 14:15; CCC 367).

5:26 a holy kiss: An outward sign of fraternal affection (Rom 16:16; 1 Pet 5:14).

5:27 I adjure you: Paul is putting his readers under oath to ensure that his written instructions are made known to every member of the Church. The eucharistic liturgy was the most suitable context for a public reading of the letter (1 Tim 4:13).

[c2] Or *with them.*

STUDY QUESTIONS
1 Thessalonians

Chapter 1

For understanding
1. **1:1.** Who are the Silvanus and Timothy mentioned in this verse? How is the Church family in Thessalonica united?
2. **1:3.** What is Paul remembering? How does each of the theological virtues apply to the Thessalonian situation?
3. **1:7.** What are Macedonia and Achaia, and where are they in relation to each other?
4. **1:9.** What does Paul's phrasing suggest about the Thessalonians' religious background? What is the traditional Jewish critique of idolatry contained in the Scriptures? In what respect is the Jewish faith the faith of the Church?

For application
1. **1:2.** When you pray, for whom do you pray? For whom should you be praying? How often do you give thanks for that person's faith in, hope for, and love of Jesus Christ and his Church?
2. **1:5.** To what extent do you experience the gospel as more than a matter of words and dogmas—as, rather, a matter of power in the Holy Spirit and utter conviction? If, as Paul suggests, the gospel should come in power, what might you do to receive it that way?
3. **1:6.** Which Catholics (living or not) do you most admire for their practice of the faith? How have you imitated those you admire? What has been the fruit of your imitation? To extend this question a little farther, how do you imitate the Lord?
4. **1:9.** To what do you devote more time and attention in everyday life than you should? Might these pursuits qualify as idols, in the sense that you spend too much energy and affection in their service? How can you turn from them to the service of a God who is a living reality in your life?

Chapter 2

For understanding
1. **2:9.** Why did Paul and his companions avoid claiming their rights to material and financial support during their brief stay with the Thessalonians? How did they support themselves?
2. **2:13.** To what does "the word of God" refer here? How was it delivered? What OT personages do the apostles and their associates parallel, and how?
3. **2:14-16.** For whom does Paul have some unusually harsh words? Why does he trace this madness to Jerusalem? Who is persecuting the Thessalonians?
4. **Word Study: At Last (2:16).** What are some of the ways this expression is used in the New Testament? If Paul's use of the expression in 1 Thessalonians is a matter of interpretation, what three possible interpretations can be given it? Why is a decision about the meaning difficult here?

For application
1. **2:1-4.** Think of someone you admire for his refusal to give up in the face of opposition. What is it about that person's attitude that you most admire? How might that attitude encourage you in the face of opposition—especially of a religious or spiritual nature?
2. **2:11-12.** If you are a parent or are responsible for children or adolescents, how do you exhort, encourage, and charge them "to lead a life worthy of God"? If you are direct and explicit, how do you respond when your charges seem to ignore or reject your encouragement? If you are indirect or "hands off", how do you know that they perceive your approach as encouragement to lead such a life?
3. **2:13.** How do you receive the Church's teaching on moral issues? Do you accept it as the word of God for you—that is, as the truth—or as someone's opinion? If you accept it as the word of God, how can you tell when it "is at work in you"? That is, what effect is it having on you?

Chapter 3

For understanding
1. **3:2.** Why did Paul send Timothy to visit the Thessalonians? When did Timothy return? What happened as a result of the visit?
2. **3:10.** What did Paul fear was lacking in the Thessalonians' faith?
3. **3:12.** When Paul talks about love in this verse, about what kind of love is he speaking? How does this kind of love function? Why can only God make this love increase and overflow?
4. **3:13.** To whom can the expression "all his saints" in this verse refer? What is Paul most likely saying? What other Scripture passages support this interpretation?

For application
1. **3:1–5.** How do you deal with uncertainty over the faith of people you love, especially if their faith is new or is undergoing trial? What steps do you take to encourage them to persevere?
2. **3:10.** Have you ever tried to instruct anyone in the faith? How did you go about it? For example, how did you determine what those you were instructing needed to know? How could you tell when they were "getting" what you were teaching and were growing in faith?
3. **3:12.** Reflect on the note for this verse. How has the Lord caused love to increase in your own life? in the lives of those you catechize?

Chapter 4

For understanding
1. **4:3.** Describe the processes of sanctification. Of what is it a condition? To what does the injunction "abstain from immorality" refer? Where did the Greek expression used here originate?
2. **4:13.** For what is "asleep" a metaphor? What does Scripture imply by using it? Though it is human to mourn for the death of a loved one, how should the Christian handle grief?
3. **4:15.** What do some scholars infer from Paul's use of "we" in this passage? What other comments in Paul's letters seem to weigh against this common interpretation?
4. **4:16–17.** What kind of imagery does Paul use to depict the Second Coming of Jesus? What three OT examples does the note cite, and for which specific images?

For application
1. **4:3–7.** Look up and read Tob 8:4–7. What is the connection between Paul's admonition and Tobias' attitude toward taking a wife? What connection is there between chastity, sexual expression within marriage, and the sanctification of the spouses?
2. **4:9–12.** At first, Paul's injunctions, on the one hand, to love the brethren and, on the other, "to live quietly, to mind your own affairs, and to work with your hands" may appear to be contradictory. How can tending to one's own work be an expression of love for the community?
3. **4:13–14.** If you have ever grieved for the loss of a loved one, how did your grief challenge your hope? How did hope reassert itself? What is the basis for Christian hope?
4. **4:15–18.** If you have ever comforted anyone who has lost a loved one, what kinds of comfort did you offer? How was it received? How would you want to be comforted in a similar situation?

Chapter 5

For understanding

1. **5:2**. What is the "day of the Lord", and what does Paul know about it? How does the liturgy anticipate this final and fateful day? How is it prefigured in history?
2. **5:5**. What is the Semitic expression "sons of light" a way of saying? To what does the struggle between light and darkness refer, and where do you find it discussed in Jewish tradition?
3. **5:12**. What does the expression "over you in the Lord" indicate about the Thessalonian Church? Why is this situation not surprising? To what does the spiritual oversight of these pastors entitle them from the laity?
4. **5:23.** In using the formula "spirit and soul and body", what is Paul emphasizing? What is he *not* intending to emphasize? What distinctions *can* be made among these components?

For application

1. **5:1–4.** How predictable is your life? How far into the future do you tend to make plans? What do these verses suggest for the ways you should be planning?
2. **5:5–8a.** What kind of sobriety do you think Paul is talking about here? What does drunkenness represent (beyond an excess of alcohol)? How do these verses compare with what Paul said in 4:3 about sanctification?
3. **5:12–13a.** Why are bishops and pastors always entitled to your respect? In what ways have you personally shown respect to them, especially around others? How often do you pray for them?
4. **5:16–18.** Since Paul advises rejoicing, prayer, and thanksgiving "in all circumstances" as God's will for you, how do you act on his advice? What does it mean to rejoice or give thanks when times are tough? How do you pray constantly?
5. **5:19–24.** Read these verses slowly, with an emphasis on v. 24. How secure is your confidence that God is faithful to you and will (note the definite future) sanctify you if you cooperate with him?

INTRODUCTION TO THE
SECOND LETTER OF SAINT PAUL TO THE THESSALONIANS

Author   Second Thessalonians is a genuine letter from the Apostle Paul. His name stands at the beginning of it (1:1); his personal signature stands at the end of it (3:17); and Christian tradition has universally accepted its authenticity from earliest times. Despite this, a surprising number of scholars have come to doubt or even deny the apostolic authorship of 2 Thessalonians. They claim instead that an admirer of Paul, hiding behind the name of the apostle, penned the epistle toward the end of the first century. Among other things, the argument is made (1) that 2 Thessalonians has a different perspective on the timing of Christ's return (still distant) from that of 1 Thessalonians (imminent) and (2) that the remarkable similarities between 1 and 2 Thessalonians raise suspicions that the second letter was written in conscious imitation of the first. Neither of these objections is sufficiently strong to topple the traditional view. On the timing of Christ's coming, it must be stressed that Paul never claimed in 1 Thessalonians that Jesus would return immediately, only that he would come suddenly (1 Thess 5:2). This, it would seem, is the very misunderstanding that Paul sets out to correct in 2 Thessalonians (2:1–3). On the similarities between the two epistles, it must be recognized that Paul's distinctive style is a blade that cuts both ways. In theory, similarities of expression could mean that someone was trying to imitate Paul; but it is far more natural to suppose that the apostle himself was simply writing in his usual style. Finally, it would be exceedingly odd for someone impersonating Paul to warn the Thessalonians not to accept fabricated letters purporting to come from the apostle (2:2). For the use of the plural "we" and "us" throughout the letter (1:3, 11; 2:1; 3:1; etc.), see the introduction to First Thessalonians: *Author.*

Date and Destination   Scholars who hold the traditional view of Pauline authorship agree that 2 Thessalonians was written about the same time (A.D. 50 or 51) and probably from the same place (Corinth) as 1 Thessalonians. Reference is made to the first epistle in 2:15, but it is uncertain how much earlier it was sent off. The situation of the Church seems to be the same, and Paul's focus on the return of Jesus in both letters suggests the second could have been written within weeks or months of the first. In any case, both Thessalonian letters were sent to the same Church in Macedonia (northern Greece) that Paul and his coworkers had founded on his second missionary tour (Acts 17:1–9). See introduction to First Thessalonians: *Destination.*

Purpose and Themes   Paul sent 2 Thessalonians as a follow-up letter to 1 Thessalonians, which was partly ignored and partly misunderstood by his readers. There was need now to correct the way certain believers were thinking and living in light of Christ's expected return. The letter addresses this twofold problem with doctrinal exposition and moral exhortation. **(1)** *Doctrinal Exposition.* As in his first letter, Paul gives readers an eschatological vision of things to come. This is necessary because some of the Thessalonians are shaken by an alarming idea, based on a misunderstanding of his first letter (1 Thess 4:13—5:12) and reinforced by another letter forged in Paul's name (2:2), that the end times have arrived and the Second Coming of Jesus is just around the corner. Paul considers this a deception (2:3) because Christ will not return in glory until a whole series of events have taken place first. Specifically, Paul insists that a nefarious "man of lawlessness", an agent of Satan, must first be allowed to spread confusion throughout the world and impress the wicked with signs and wonders of his power (2:3, 9–10). This villain has yet to arrive because a mysterious force restrains him from showing his face until the appointed time (2:7–8). Only after this period of turmoil and tribulation will Christ come again as the divine Warrior and Judge to slay the offender and condemn the ungodly (2:8). **(2)** *Moral Exhortation.* Confusion about the timing of Christ's coming has led certain believers into strange and disorderly conduct. We can infer from Paul's comments in 3:6–15 that some in Thessalonica were so convinced that Jesus would return at any moment that they had quit their jobs and stopped working for a living. Paul has nothing good to say about this behavior and seems annoyed that his readers have not heeded his earlier appeals to "work" diligently (1 Thess 4:11) and "admonish the idle" (1 Thess 5:14). The congregation is charged with addressing this problem decisively but charitably (3:14–15). In Paul's mind, these freeloaders who live on the charity of others will better prepare themselves for Christ's return by working than by sitting around waiting.

OUTLINE OF THE SECOND LETTER OF SAINT PAUL TO THE THESSALONIANS

1. **Opening Address (1:1–2)**

2. **Personal Encouragement from Paul (1:3–12)**
   A. Thanksgiving (1:3–4)
   B. The Day of Judgment (1:5–10)
   C. Prayer for Spiritual Progress (1:11–12)

3. **The Coming Day of the Lord (2:1–17)**
   A. The Rebellion Comes First (2:1–12)
   B. Thanksgiving and Appeal (2:13–15)
   C. Prayer for Comfort (2:16–17)

4. **Exhortations to Love and Labor (3:1–15)**
   A. Prayers for and from Paul (3:1–5)
   B. Admonishing the Idle (3:6–15)

5. **Conclusion (3:16–18)**

THE SECOND LETTER OF SAINT PAUL TO THE

THESSALONIANS

Salutation

1 Paul, Silva'nus, and Timothy,
  To the Church of the Thessalo'nians in God our Father and the Lord Jesus Christ:
2 Grace to you and peace from God the Father and the Lord Jesus Christ.

Thanksgiving

3 We are bound to give thanks to God always for you, brethren, as is fitting, because your faith is growing abundantly, and the love of every one of you for one another is increasing. ⁴Therefore we ourselves boast of you in the churches of God for your steadfastness and faith in all your persecutions and in the afflictions which you are enduring.

The Judgment at Christ's Coming

5 This is evidence of the righteous judgment of God, that you may be made worthy of the kingdom of God, for which you are suffering—⁶since indeed God deems it just to repay with affliction those who afflict you, ⁷and to grant rest with us to you who are afflicted, when the Lord Jesus is revealed from heaven with his mighty angels in flaming fire, ⁸inflicting vengeance upon those who do not know God and upon those who do not obey the gospel of our Lord Jesus. ⁹They shall suffer the punishment of eternal destruction and exclusion from the presence of the Lord and from the glory of his might, ¹⁰when he comes on that day to be glorified in his saints, and to be marveled at in all

---

1:1: 1 Thess 1:1; 2 Cor 1:19; Acts 16:1.
1:2: Rom 1:7. **1:3:** 1 Thess 1:2. **1:8:** Gal 4:8.

1:1 Paul, Silvanus, and Timothy: The missionaries who founded the Church in Thessalonica. This is the second epistle they have sent to the congregation. See note on 1 Thess 1:1.

1:1-2 Paul describes the relation between God and the Thessalonian Church with two small but significant prepositions. Believers are united **in** the Father and the Son (1:1) by the grace and peace that come **from** the Father and the Son (1:2). In effect, the triune God is both the locus and source of every spiritual blessing (Eph 1:3-14).

1:2 Grace to you and peace: An early Christian greeting used by Paul and other NT writers (1 Pet 1:2; 2 Jn 3; Rev 1:4).

1:3 give thanks: Nearly every Pauline epistle opens with words of gratitude (Rom 1:8; 1 Cor 1:4; etc.). His thankfulness rises to God for the Thessalonians because their **faith** and **love** are growing steadily in direct answer to his prayers (1 Thess 3:12).

1:4 your persecutions: Trials began within weeks of Paul's arrival in Thessalonica when a band of embittered Jews instigated an uproar against the apostle, his missionary team, and their friends (Acts 17:5-9). Local antagonism has continued unabated since then (1 Thess 1:6; 2:14). Paul is proud to advertise how well the young Church is weathering these storms.

1:5-10 An apocalyptic preview of the Day of Judgment. Here Paul focuses on the outcome of the proceedings rather than the process: to the saints, Christ will give eternal life and rest, but to sinners, he will give a sentence of eternal death and retribution. This closing act of human history will forever separate the sheep and the goats, sending them their separate ways (Mt 25:31-46; CCC 1038-41). See note on Rom 2:6.

1:5 This is evidence: Even before the Judgment, clear distinctions between the righteous and the wicked are emerging in Thessalonica: on one side, believers are suffering and yet

holding fast to their faith; on the other, persecutors are harassing and abusing them in godless ways. This is a sign of blessedness for Paul's readers (Mt 5:9-10) and a frightening omen for their oppressors (2 Cor 2:15-16). **righteous judgment:** God will judge the world through Christ (Acts 17:31) with perfect justice and impartiality (Rom 2:9-11; 1 Pet 2:23; CCC 682). **the kingdom of God:** The heavenly inheritance of the saints. In Paul's theology, fidelity through suffering is a means of sanctification, i.e., it helps to make us worthy of the kingdom (Acts 14:22; Rom 8:17). See note on 1 Thess 2:12.

1:7 flaming fire: Symbolic of divine scrutiny and judgment (Is 66:16; 1 Cor 3:13-15).

1:8 inflicting vengeance: Assurance that Christ will right every wrong and repay the wicked for their malice should encourage believers to refrain from avenging themselves by personal retaliation (Rom 12:19; 1 Thess 5:15). **do not know God:** Unenlightened pagans (1 Thess 4:5). **do not obey the gospel:** Such as the unbelievers of Israel (Rom 10:16).

1:9 eternal destruction: Not annihilation or the termination of existence, but an everlasting state of spiritual death, disinheritance, and damnation. For Paul, hell is nothing less than eternal separation from the peace and presence of the living God. Other biblical ideas and images fill out the picture of this terrifying prospect: the damned will endure "tribulation and distress" (Rom 2:9), "eternal punishment" (Mt 25:46), and "unquenchable fire" (Lk 3:17; Is 66:24) (CCC 1033-36). See word study: *Hell* at Mk 9:43.

1:10 that day: The final "day of the Lord" (2:2). **his saints:** Or, "his holy ones". This could refer to the redeemed People of God (Jude), but it is more likely a reference to the holy angels (1:7; Ps 89:7). Either way, their appearance in glory will magnify the glory of Christ, whose divine splendor shines through them (Phil 3:21; Col 3:4). See note on 1 Thess 3:13.

who have believed, because our testimony to you was believed. ¹¹To this end we always pray for you, that our God may make you worthy of his call, and may fulfil every good resolve and work of faith by his power, ¹²so that the name of our Lord Jesus may be glorified in you, and you in him, according to the grace of our God and the Lord Jesus Christ.

The Man of Lawlessness

2 Now concerning the coming of our Lord Jesus Christ and our assembling to meet him, we beg you, brethren, ²not to be quickly shaken in mind or excited, either by spirit or by word, or by letter purporting to be from us, to the effect that the day of the Lord has come. ³Let no one deceive you in any way; for that day will not come, unless the rebellion comes first, and the man of lawlessness ᵃ is revealed, the son of perdition, ⁴who opposes and exalts himself against every so-called god or object of worship, so that he takes his seat in the temple of God, proclaiming himself to be God. ⁵Do you not remember that when I was still with you I told you this? ⁶And you know what is restraining him now so that he may be revealed in his time. ⁷For the mystery of lawlessness is already at work; only he who now restrains it will do so until he is out of the

---

1:11: 1 Thess 1:3.   **2:1:** 1 Thess 4:15–17.   **2:2:** 2 Thess 3:17.
2:3: Eph 5:6–8; Dan 7:25; 8:25; 11:36; Rev 13:5; Jn 17:12.   **2:4:** Ezek 28:2.
2:5: 1 Thess 3:4.

1:11 we always pray: Paul and his coworkers practice what they preach on the subject of continuous prayer (1 Thess 5:17).

1:12 our God and the Lord Jesus Christ: Several times Paul mentions the close relationship between the Father and the Son in his Thessalonian letters (1:1, 2; 2:16; 1 Thess 1:1; 3:11).

2:1–12 Paul combats misinformation in Thessalonica that the day of the Second Coming is at hand. This appears to be the teaching of doomsday prophets who may have gotten the idea from a misreading of 1 Thessalonians (especially 1 Thess 5:2). In any case, they apparently forged a letter to this effect in Paul's name and claimed to have had personal revelations to back it up. To silence these troublemakers and steady his shaken readers, Paul lays out the eschatological sequence of events that must take place *before* the "day of the Lord" dawns on the world (2:2). Though the basic outline of this prophecy is clear, no clear consensus exists in ancient or modern scholarship on how to understand many of its details (CCC 673-74).

2:1 the coming of our Lord: The return of Christ, who will come again in glory (Acts 1:11) to judge the living and the dead (Acts 10:42). **our assembling:** Believers, both living and deceased, will be taken up with the Lord into heavenly glory (1 Thess 4:16-17).

2:2 shaken . . . or excited: False prophets are unsettling Paul's readers, whose suffering and affliction seem to reinforce allegations that the tribulation of the last days is under way and is about to give way to the Second Coming (1:6; 1 Thess 2:14). **by spirit or by word:** I.e., by charismatic revelations. These need to be measured against apostolic teaching in order to test their authenticity (1 Cor 14:29; 1 Thess 5:20-21). **by letter:** I.e., by a forged document claiming to come from Paul, Silvanus, and Timothy (1:1). Paul considers this a form of deception (2:3). **the day of the Lord:** The Day of Judgment. See note on 1 Thess 5:2.

2:3 the rebellion: Or, "the apostasy". Paul envisions a time of terrible confusion and massive falling away from God at the end of days (1 Tim 4:1-2; 2 Tim 3:1-5). **the man of lawlessness:** A man of extraordinary evil. When he comes, he will *deify* himself, claiming to be God (2:4); he will *dazzle* the wicked with displays of his power (2:9); and he will *deceive* the world with falsehoods of every kind (2:10). Most identify this figure with "the antichrist" prophesied by John (1 Jn 2:18, 22; 4:3; 2 Jn 1:7) (CCC 675-77). **son of perdition:** A Semitic way of saying "one who is doomed to destruction". Jesus gave this title to his betrayer, Judas Iscariot (Jn 17:12).

2:4 exalts himself: The Antichrist will declare himself God and demand to be worshiped. This point is identified differently by different interpreters. **(1)** Some (e.g., St. Irenaeus, St. Cyril of Jerusalem) see it as a reference to the Jerusalem Temple. This view entails a belief that the sanctuary, which now lies in ruins, will be rebuilt in the end times. **(2)** Oth-

ers (e.g., St. John Chrysostom, St. Ephraem the Syrian) see a reference to the Church, since in Paul's theology, believers make up the true Temple of God (1 Cor 3:16; 2 Cor 6:16; Eph 2:21). **(3)** It is also possible to understand the expression metaphorically, i.e., as a visual description of the Antichrist's supreme arrogance in putting himself in the place of God. ● Paul's portrait of the Antichrist is modeled on the blasphemous villains of biblical history, such as the king of Babylon, who wanted to make himself like the Most High and sit enthroned in heaven (Is 14:13-14), the prince of Tyre, who claimed to be a god and sit in the seat of the gods (Ezek 28:2), and the Syrian ruler Antiochus Epiphanes IV, who exalted himself above every god and desecrated the Jerusalem Temple with a pagan altar and idol (Dan 11:36; 1 Mac 1:20-24, 54).

2:7 mystery of lawlessness: The secret operation of evil in the world. Readers are already getting a taste of this through the bitter experience of persecution (1:4). The steady build-up

---

Word Study

Restraining (2 Thess 2:6)

Katechō (Gk.): a verb meaning "hinder", "restrain", or "retain". It is used three times in the Thessalonian letters and 14 times elsewhere in the NT. Its usage in 2 Thessalonians is challenging to interpret. In 2 Thess 2:6, Paul speaks of a mysterious *power* (neuter) that holds back the man of lawlessness and delays his appearance in the world. Then, in 2 Thess 2:7, he seems to speak of a *person* (masculine) who performs this function until, at last, he steps out of the way and the man of lawlessness makes his terrifying debut. The identities of this force and figure have been greatly debated in both ancient and modern times. For many, the restraining power is the law and order enforced by the Roman Empire, and the restrainer is the Roman emperor himself. Others contend that the Holy Spirit (neuter in Greek) is the restraining power and that God the Father (masculine in Greek) is the Person who issues the restraining order. Still others interpret the restraining force as the missionary efforts of the Church and the figure who embodies this mission as Paul. Unfortunately for us, Paul felt no need to describe further the restrainer because he had already instructed his readers on this point when he was with them in person (2 Thess 2:5-6).

ᵃ Other ancient authorities read *sin*.

way. [8]And then the lawless one will be revealed, and the Lord Jesus will slay him with the breath of his mouth and destroy him by his appearing and his coming. [9]The coming of the lawless one by the activity of Satan will be with all power and with pretended signs and wonders, [10]and with all wicked deception for those who are to perish, because they refused to love the truth and so be saved. [11]Therefore God sends upon them a strong delusion, to make them believe what is false, [12]so that all may be condemned who did not believe the truth but had pleasure in unrighteousness.

Chosen for Salvation

13 But we are bound to give thanks to God always for you, brethren beloved by the Lord, because God chose you from the beginning[b] to be saved through sanctification by the Spirit[c] and belief in the truth. [14]To this he called you through our gospel, so that you may obtain the glory of our Lord Jesus Christ. [15]So then, brethren, stand firm and hold to the traditions which you were taught by us, either by word of mouth or by letter.

16 Now may our Lord Jesus Christ himself, and God our Father, who loved us and gave us eternal comfort and good hope through grace, [17]comfort your hearts and establish them in every good work and word.

Request for Prayer

3 Finally, brethren, pray for us, that the word of the Lord may speed on and triumph, as it did among you, [2]and that we may be delivered from wicked and evil men; for not all have faith. [3]But the Lord is faithful; he will strengthen you and guard you from evil.[d] [4]And we have confidence in the Lord about you, that you are doing and will do the things which we command. [5]May the Lord direct your hearts to the love of God and to the steadfastness of Christ.

Warning against Idleness

6 Now we command you, brethren, in the name of our Lord Jesus Christ, that you keep away from any brother who is walking in idleness and not in accord with the tradition that you received from us. [7]For you yourselves know how you ought to imitate us; we were not idle when we were with you, [8]we did not eat any one's bread without paying, but with toil and labor we worked night and day, that we might not burden any of you. [9]It was not because we have not that right, but to give you in our conduct an example to imitate. [10]For even when we were with you, we gave you this

---

2:8: Is 11:4.   **2:9:** Mt 24:24; Jn 4:48.   **2:11:** Rom 1:28.   **2:13:** 2 Thess 1:3; Eph 1:4; 1 Pet 1:2.   **2:15:** 1 Cor 16:13; 11:2.
          2:16: 1 Thess 3:11; 1 Pet 1:3.   **3:1:** 1 Thess 5:25; 1:8.   **3:2:** Rom 15:31.   **3:3:** 1 Cor 1:9; 1 Thess 5:24.
     3:6: 1 Cor 5:4, 5, 11; 1 Thess 5:14.   **3:7:** 1 Thess 1:6, 9.   **3:8:** 1 Thess 2:9; Acts 18:3; Eph 4:28.   **3:9:** 2 Thess 3:7.
                                                     3:10: 1 Thess 4:11.

---

of iniquity throughout history is paving the way for an explosion of evil in the last days (CCC 385).

2:8 Jesus will slay him: Christ will descend from heaven as a divine Warrior to destroy the man of lawlessness with a word and trample the last remnants of evil underfoot (1 Cor 15:24). **the breath of his mouth:** Or, "the Spirit of his mouth". ● Paul is alluding to Is 11:4, where the Messiah appears as a judge who vindicates the poor and oppressed and slays the wicked with his powerful word.

2:9 activity of Satan: Suggests the man of lawlessness is an instrument in the hands of the devil. **pretended signs:** Displays of demonic power that will captivate sinners and lead them blindly astray. These are not miracles in the strict sense, which are properly the work of God, but illusions that make sinners think the power of God is being witnessed.

2:11 a strong delusion: God will respond to the wicked by worsening their problem. Because they will defy God and willfully reject the truth, he will permit them to love their evils and errors without the merciful restraint of his grace (Is 6:9-10; 29:9-10). See note on Rom 1:24. ● Paul says "God will send" because, by his own just judgment, God will permit the devil to do these things. Being judged in this way, sinners will be deceived; and being deceived, they will be judged (St. Augustine, *City of God* 20, 19).

2:13 God chose you: By an eternal decree of love (Eph 1:5). **sanctification:** The processes of becoming "holy", which Paul naturally links with the Holy Spirit's work within us. See note on 1 Thess 4:3.

2:15 the traditions: The teaching that Paul handed over to his readers, whether in writing or by oral instruction. This was the standard against which doctrinal claims (2:5) and moral behavior (3:6) were to be measured and judged. Even

Paul's personal example was a form of apostolic catechesis (3:7-9; 1 Cor 11:2; 2 Tim 1:13) (CCC 75-76, 82). ● The apostles did not hand down everything in writing; many unwritten things were handed down as well, and both written and unwritten are worthy of belief. So let us also regard the tradition of the Church as worthy of belief (St. John Chrysostom, *Homilies on 2 Thessalonians* 4).

3:1-2 Paul requests intercession for the progress of the gospel and the protection of missionaries entrusted with it. It is because Paul lived and worked in the midst of constant danger that he relied on his churches to pray for a safe and successful ministry (Rom 15:30-31; 2 Cor 1:11; 1 Thess 5:25).

3:1 the word of the Lord: The gospel message itself. See note on 1 Thess 2:13.

3:4 which we command: Whether in person (3:10) or in writing (3:6, 12).

3:6-15 Paul addresses an embarrassing situation in the Thessalonian Church. Certain believers, perhaps enamored with the idea that Christ could return at any moment, became *idlers*, who stopped working for a living, *freeloaders*, who relied on the charity of others to support themselves, and *busybodies*, who started meddling in the affairs of everyone else. Paul insists they should return to work, earn their own living, and mind their own business (3:12). He urges the Church to get involved in correcting this problem by warning such brothers (3:15) and, if necessary, shunning them if they refuse correction (3:14). See introduction: *Purpose and Themes*.

3:8 toil and labor: Paul and companions supported themselves with a trade or some other form of employment on top of their missionary work. Paul was teaching the Thessalonians by example about the dignity and necessity of human labor (CCC 2427). See notes on 1 Thess 2:9 and 4:11.

3:10 when we were . . . with you: Suggests idleness was already an issue when Paul ministered among them. This is why his earlier letter urges the Church to "admonish the idle" (1 Thess 5:14). **let him not eat:** I.e., let him not live off the

---

[b] Other ancient authorities read *as the first converts.*
[c] Or *of spirit.*
[d] Or *the Evil One.*

command: If any one will not work, let him not eat. [11]For we hear that some of you are walking in idleness, mere busybodies, not doing any work. [12]Now such persons we command and exhort in the Lord Jesus Christ to do their work in quietness and to earn their own living. [13]Brethren, do not be weary in well-doing.

14 If any one refuses to obey what we say in this letter, note that man, and have nothing to do with him, that he may be ashamed. [15]Do not look on him as an enemy, but warn him as a brother.

Final Greetings and Benediction

16 Now may the Lord of peace himself give you peace at all times in all ways. The Lord be with you all.

17 I, Paul, write this greeting with my own hand. This is the mark in every letter of mine; it is the way I write. [18]The grace of our Lord Jesus Christ be with you all.

3:11: 2 Thess 3:6. 3:12: 1 Thess 4:1, 11. 3:13: Gal 6:9. 3:16: Ruth 2:4.
3:17: 1 Cor 16:21. 3:18: Rom 16:20; 1 Thess 5:28.

---

labor of others without contributing efforts of his own.
• Manual labor aims at obtaining food, removing idleness, curbing fallen desires, and enabling almsgiving. As a means of acquiring food, work is commanded as a precept, so that one who has no other means of livelihood is bound to work. This is signified by the words of the apostle (St. Thomas Aquinas, *Summa Theologiae* II-II, 187, 3).

3:14 may be ashamed: Disciplinary exclusion from the life and liturgy of the Church would serve (1) to deter others from living or contemplating a life of idleness and (2) to induce repentance from the offenders in the hope of restoring them to full fellowship.

3:17 I, Paul, write this: Paul takes up the pen to write the final greeting with his own hand, having dictated the rest of the letter to a secretary. His personal signature and remarks authenticate the epistle as a genuine apostolic work (1 Cor 16:21; Col 4:18). He stresses the point here because the Thessalonians may have received a forged letter that alleged to be from Paul but was not (2:2). **every letter of mine:** Implies that Paul was in the habit of sending out letters. The statement strikes many scholars as odd, since the Thessalonian letters are the two earliest NT writings that come from Paul. Some take this as evidence that someone other than the apostle—most likely a later disciple, familiar with the corpus of Pauline epistles—must be the real author of this letter. The argument is ingenious, but it must be remembered that not all of Paul's correspondence necessarily made its way into the collection of NT books. It is possible that some of his letters were neither canonized nor preserved (see, e.g., 1 Cor 5:9 and Col 4:16). The existence of noncanonical letters written during Paul's early ministry is not established with certainty, but it cannot be ruled out.

STUDY QUESTIONS
2 Thessalonians

Chapter 1

For understanding
1. **1:1–2.** With what two small but significant prepositions does Paul express the relationship between God and the Thessalonian Church? What does the triune God represent for Paul in connection with every spiritual blessing?
2. **1:5–10.** What do these verses provide? What is Paul's focus here?
3. **1:9.** To what does the expression "eternal destruction" refer? What is *hell* in Paul's thinking? What other New Testament ideas and images fill out this terrifying prospect?
4. **1:12.** What does Paul frequently mention in the two Thessalonian letters regarding the Father and the Son?

For application
1. **1:4–5.** Why do Christians pass around stories of groups (other than their own) that have endured hardship or persecution? Why do you think the Catholic Church takes such an interest in martyrologies (collections of stories about martyrs)?
2. **1:6–8.** As you read these verses, what tone of voice do you "hear"? Why do you think Paul would wish for divine vengeance to fall on people who do not know God? (Then again, what is "knowing God" in Paul's language?) How are failure to know God and disobedience related here?
3. **1:9.** Having considered the note for this verse, what is your own belief concerning the existence and nature of hell? What do you know of the Church's current teaching about hell and those who go there? (Refer to CCC 1033–36.) If you have difficulty with that teaching, what is the basis for the difficulty?
4. **1:11.** According to this verse, how does God fulfill our resolves and good works of faith? Why are good resolutions and good works (even ones done in faith) not enough by themselves?

Chapter 2

For understanding
1. **2:3.** What is another word for "rebellion" here? What is Paul envisioning? Who is the "man of lawlessness", also called the "son of perdition"?
2. **Word Study: Restraining (2:6).** The note points out that the term "restrain" in 2 Thessalonians is difficult to interpret. Remembering that Greek words have gender, what do the *power* (neuter) and the *person* (masculine) do? What or who have they been thought to be? Why did Paul feel no need to describe the restrainer further?
3. **2:7.** What is the "mystery of lawlessness"? Toward what is it building?
4. **2:15.** What are the "traditions" to which Paul refers? What did the traditions serve as a standard for judging? What role did Paul's personal example of Christian living serve?

For application
1. **2:3–4.** Given the events of the last hundred years, several historical figures might easily fit this description. How would you avoid letting yourself be deceived by a charismatic but devious personality? (Hint: Look ahead to verse 15.) How would you prevent others from being deceived?
2. **2:10–12.** In these verses, what sort of person will be condemned? Why? How can someone "take pleasure in unrighteousness"?
3. **2:13.** What were you chosen by God to do? When? How is this choice the opposite of what happens in the previous verse?
4. **2:14–15.** Why is it important to "hold fast" to the deposit of faith? If someone were to urge you to "question" Church teaching, what would that person actually be urging you to do? What *should* be the effect of asking questions of this deposit of faith so as to understand it better?

Chapter 3

For understanding

1. **3:1–2.** For what purpose is Paul soliciting intercessory prayer from the Thessalonian Church?
2. **3:6–15.** What embarrassing situation in the Thessalonian Church is Paul addressing? What three groups of people is he talking about? How does he urge the Church to get involved in correcting this problem?
3. **3:14.** What two purposes did Paul expect disciplinary exclusion from the life and liturgy of the Church to serve?
4. **3:17.** Why did Paul, having dictated the letter to a secretary, take up his pen and add his own signature and some personal remarks at the end?

For application

1. **3:3.** What is Paul promising you here? How does your faith both strengthen you and "guard you from evil"? Assuming he does not mean that God will prevent evil from happening, what kind of "guard" might Paul be talking about?
2. **3:6–10.** Paul seems to advocate a kind of "tough love" here. When is it appropriate to help someone who is not working, and when is it appropriate not to help such a person? How do you seek help from the Christian community when you are in trouble yourself?
3. **3:13.** Have you ever become tired of living the Christian life? What might cause such a weariness? What prompts or encourages you to "keep on keeping on"?
4. **3:14–15.** If a fellow Christian is publicly dissenting from the faith or practice of the Church, how do you treat him, not as an enemy, but as a brother? Why might Paul recommend that you avoid his company? How would you go about warning him without being sanctimonious about it?

INTRODUCTION TO THE
FIRST LETTER OF SAINT PAUL TO TIMOTHY

Author First Timothy purports to be a letter from the Apostle Paul (1:1), as do the letters of 2 Timothy (2 Tim 1:1) and Titus (Tit 1:1). These three epistles, closely related to one another in theme and purpose, are collectively known as the Pastoral Epistles. From earliest times, Christians accepted these letters as authentic compositions of Paul. Bishops such as Clement of Rome (A.D. 95) and Polycarp (A.D. 120) allude to the Pastoral Epistles as genuine Pauline writings, and later theologians such as Irenaeus (A.D. 180), Tertullian (A.D. 200), and Clement of Alexandria (A.D. 200) make direct assertions to this effect.

Despite the constancy of this view in early Christian times, the tradition of Pauline authorship came under fire in the nineteenth century. Increasingly scholars began to regard the Pastoral Epistles as pseudepigraphical letters that were written in Paul's name by one or more of his disciples several decades after his death. This position, which continues to dominate much of modern scholarship, contends that the Pastoral Epistles are conspicuously different from Paul's undisputed letters in vocabulary, style, and emphasis, and for this reason, they cannot be regarded as genuine writings of the apostle. Regarding their historical content, some insist these writings bear witness to an advanced stage of Church government that did not exist in Paul's day and that the details they claim to provide of Paul's missionary efforts are inconsistent with his travels known from the Book of Acts and the other Pauline epistles. These and other arguments provide the basis for the pseudepigraphical hypothesis.

That being said, the distinctiveness of the Pastoral Epistles is a factor that must be weighed carefully, for the evidence can be interpreted in different ways. For instance, even critics who deny Pauline authorship generally recognize traces of Paul's thinking throughout these letters, and this leaves open the possibility of a closer relationship to the apostle than that envisioned by pseudepigraphical advocates. Stylistic differences between the Pastorals and Paul's undisputed writings, while undeniable, probably have more to do with differences in purpose and subject matter than anything else. After all, the Pastoral Epistles are written to pastors (Timothy and Titus) who are already well-seasoned and educated leaders in the Church, while Paul's other letters are written to instruct young congregations in the basics of Christian faith. Allegations that the ecclesiastical hierarchy outlined in the Pastorals was unknown to the Church of Paul's day are likewise overdrawn, since several passages in the undisputed letters of Paul point to a structured system of leadership already in place during the earliest days of the Church (1 Cor 12:28; Phil 1:1; 1 Thess 5:12; cf. Acts 14:23; 20:17). As for Paul's travel itinerary, one must admit that these letters claim to give us information about Paul's career that is otherwise uncorroborated in the NT. Nevertheless, this can be taken as an earmark of Pauline authorship, since it is more likely that a literary forgery would stay within the outline of Paul's life set forth in the Book of Acts and his genuine letters rather than depart from it. Otherwise, the attempt to pass off these letters as authentic Pauline writings would surely fail to convince the original recipients that they were reading the words of the apostle. In the end, the case against Pauline authorship is neither airtight nor immune to criticism, and the tradition that Paul himself composed the Pastoral Epistles can still be critically and convincingly defended.

Date Proponents of Pauline authorship generally date 1 Timothy in the mid 60s, between Paul's first Roman imprisonment (A.D. 60 to 62) and his martyrdom at the hands of Emperor Nero (ca. A.D. 67). It is likely that during this intervening time Paul resumed his missionary activities in the eastern parts of the Roman world and then turned his attention west toward a new mission in the province of Spain (Rom 15:24). Timothy's placement in "Ephesus" and Paul's movements in "Macedonia" put the letter somewhere in the eastern phase of this period (1:3). Scholars who deny the Pauline authorship of 1 Timothy date it much later, between A.D. 80 and 110.

Destination and Themes The letter was written to Paul's associate Timothy, who was stationed in Ephesus on special assignment (1:3). The Ephesian Church was at this time threatened by a serious pastoral crisis, with teachers and shepherds leading the flock away from the certainties of divine revelation into the mists of conjecture and speculation (1:3–7; 6:3–5). Timothy was charged with the difficult task of repairing the damage done by these troublemakers, two of whom Paul was forced to excommunicate (1:20) when he passed through on his way to Macedonia (1:3). Unable to return immediately, Paul wrote to admonish Timothy and authorize his mission to help this struggling congregation to safety.

The bulk of the letter, which is personal in tone

and informal in arrangement, covers the gamut of Timothy's pastoral responsibilities. Paul was counting on him to stabilize the Church with sound doctrine (4:6–7; 6:20) and the appointment of reliable pastors to shepherd the flock (3:1–13; 5:22). Among the congregation, he was to encourage prayer (2:1–8), set limits on the dress and conduct of women (2:9–15), attend to his liturgical duties (4:13), show respect for parishioners of all ages (5:1–2), manage the support of widows (5:3–16), take a public stand against wrongdoers (5:20), and, above all, keep himself unstained by sin (4:12; 5:22; 6:11–14). As a loyal friend and traveling assistant of the apostle, Timothy was well suited for this task, as he had been sent on previous assignments to other young Churches in Corinth (1 Cor 4:17), Philippi (Phil 2:19), and Thessalonica (1 Thess 3:2).

OUTLINE OF THE FIRST LETTER OF SAINT PAUL TO TIMOTHY

1. **Opening Address (1:1–2)**

2. **False Teaching in Ephesus (1:3–11)**
   A. Speculation and God's Law (1:3–7)
   B. The True Purpose of the Law (1:8–11)

3. **Paul's Conversion and Charge (1:12–20)**

4. **Paul's Pastoral Instructions (2:1—6:2)**
   A. Prayer and Intercession in Christ (2:1–7)
   B. Men and Women in the Liturgy (2:8–15)
   C. Ordaining Bishops and Deacons (3:1–13)
   D. Timothy as Teacher and Shepherd (3:14—4:16)
   E. Ministering to Widows, Elders, and Slaves (5:1—6:2)

5. **Final Admonitions (6:3–19)**
   A. The Dangers of Error and Wealth (6:3–10)
   B. Faithfulness and Generosity (6:11–19)

6. **Closing Appeal (6:20–21)**

THE FIRST LETTER OF SAINT PAUL TO
TIMOTHY

Salutation

1 Paul, an apostle of Christ Jesus by command of God our Savior and of Christ Jesus our hope,

2 To Timothy, my true child in the faith:

Grace, mercy, and peace from God the Father and Christ Jesus our Lord.

Warning against False Teachers

3 As I urged you when I was going to Macedonia, remain at Ephesus that you may charge certain persons not to teach any different doctrine, [4]nor to occupy themselves with myths and endless genealogies which promote speculations rather than the divine training [a] that is in faith; [5]whereas the aim of our charge is love that issues from a pure heart and a good conscience and sincere faith. [6]Certain persons by swerving from these have wandered away into vain discussion, [7]desiring to be teachers of the law, without understanding either what they are saying or the things about which they make assertions.

8 Now we know that the law is good, if any one uses it lawfully, [9]understanding this, that the law is not laid down for the just but for the lawless and disobedient, for the ungodly and sinners, for the unholy and profane, for murderers of fathers and murderers of mothers, for manslayers, [10]immoral persons, sodomites, kidnapers, liars, perjurers, and whatever else is contrary to sound doctrine, [11]in

---

1:1 Paul: The sender of the letter, traditionally identified as the great apostle to the Gentiles (2:7; Rom 11:13). As an ambassador of Christ Jesus, Paul is divinely authorized to announce the gospel to Israel and all nations (Acts 9:15). His mission stems, not from his own initiative, but from a direct command of the risen Lord (Gal 1:1, 15–16). **our Savior:** Six times in the Pastoral Epistles this title is given to God the Father (2:3; 4:10; Tit 1:3; 2:10; 3:4), and four times to Jesus Christ (2 Tim 1:10; Tit 1:4; 2:13; 3:6).

1:2 Timothy: One of Paul's associates and a member of his missionary team. He was a native of Asia Minor instructed in the Scriptures by his Jewish mother, Eunice (2 Tim 1:5; 3:15). After his conversion, Paul recruited Timothy as a traveling companion (Acts 16:1–3) and ordained him to the priestly ministry (4:14; 2 Tim 1:6). Thereafter, Timothy spent most of his time at Paul's side, as suggested by the six NT letters that identify him as a co-sender with the apostle (2 Cor; Phil; Col; 1 and 2 Thess; Philem). Though Timothy's youth might sometimes have been a liability (4:12), his health unstable (5:23), and his disposition timid and unassertive (2 Tim 1:7), Paul always thought very highly of him and considered him a dear friend (Phil 2:19–23). According to tradition, Timothy was the first bishop of Ephesus and was martyred there in old age. **my true child:** Similar expressions occur in 1:18, Phil 2:22, and 2 Tim 1:2. They imply that Paul's apostleship is a ministry of spiritual fatherhood: through preaching and administering the sacraments, he begets the supernatural life of God in others and makes them his children. Timothy is a spiritual son who received the priesthood through Paul (2 Tim 1:6), and, as the apostle's successor, he is to communicate the gift of that ministry to others as well (5:22; 2 Tim 2:1-2). See note on 1 Cor 4:15.

1:3–11 Timothy's first assignment is to halt the spread of false teaching in Ephesus (1:3). Proponents of these novelties are not missionary invaders but misguided individuals from within the Ephesian congregation. Aspiring to be teachers of the Torah (1:7), they occupy themselves with imaginative theories about the mysteries and genealogies of the books of Moses (1:4). Timothy is to silence them and preach sound doctrine

that inspires love and faith (1:5). For Paul, it is unbecoming for teachers of the faith to neglect the certainties of revelation in order to revel in the uncertainties of speculation.

1:3 Macedonia: A Roman province in northern Greece. **Ephesus:** Capital of the Roman province of Asia (Minor) in southwest Turkey. Paul established the Church there in the mid 50s on his third missionary tour (Acts 19:1—20:1). Although Ephesus is a flourishing center of Christianity in the first century, the apostle foresees doctrinal troubles heading their way (Acts 20:17, 28–29).

1:4 myths: Probably legendary stories about OT figures that are found in Jewish apocryphal writings before the dawn of Christianity (Tit 1:14). **divine training:** The Greek *oikonomia* can also mean "arrangement of God" or "household management of God". The latter sense would connect with a theme developed later in the letter, namely, that the Church is the "household" of God (3:15).

1:7 teachers of the law: Elsewhere in the NT this title is used of scribal (Lk 5:17) and rabbinic teachers (Acts 5:34).

1:8 the law: The Torah or Law of Moses is "good" because it promotes virtue and prohibits vice (Rom 7:12, 16). Since many of the sins in the following verses are direct violations of the Decalogue (Ex 20:1–17), it is clear that the moral precepts of the Old Covenant are carried over into the New and, in Paul's mind, are part of what constitutes "sound doctrine" (1:10). This is consistent with his teaching elsewhere in Rom 13:8-10, 1 Cor 7:19, and Gal 5:14. **lawfully:** I.e., according to its true intent. Improper use of the Law was made by false teachers, whose useless conjectures spread confusion instead of religious conviction among believers. The purpose of the Torah is not to satisfy our curiosity but to encourage justice, mercy, and faith (Mt 23:23) (CCC 1962). ● The person who thinks he understands the Scriptures but is unable to build up the double love of God and neighbor does not truly understand them (St. Augustine, *On Christian Doctrine* 1, 36).

1:9 for the lawless: I.e., for those who need moral direction and restraint in order to become just.

1:10 immoral persons: Literally, "fornicators". **sodomites:** The Greek refers to "male homosexuals", i.e., men who perform sexual acts with other men. For Paul's condemnation of this perversity, see Rom 1:26-27 and 1 Cor 6:9.

---

[a] Or *stewardship*, or *order*.

35

accordance with the glorious gospel of the blessed God with which I have been entrusted.

Gratitude for Mercy

12 I thank him who has given me strength for this, Christ Jesus our Lord, because he judged me faithful by appointing me to his service, [13]though I formerly blasphemed and persecuted and insulted him; but I received mercy because I had acted ignorantly in unbelief, [14]and the grace of our Lord overflowed for me with the faith and love that are in Christ Jesus. [15]The saying is sure and worthy of full acceptance, that Christ Jesus came into the world to save sinners. And I am the foremost of sinners; [16]but I received mercy for this reason, that in me, as the foremost, Jesus Christ might display his perfect patience for an example to those who were to believe in him for eternal life. [17]To the King of ages, immortal, invisible, the only God, be honor and glory for ever and ever. [b] Amen.

18 This charge I commit to you, Timothy, my son, in accordance with the prophetic utterances which pointed to you, that inspired by them you may wage the good warfare, [19]holding faith and a good conscience. By rejecting conscience, certain persons have made shipwreck of their faith, [20]among them Hymenae′us and Alexander, whom I have delivered to Satan that they may learn not to blaspheme.

Instructions concerning Prayer

2 First of all, then, I urge that supplications, prayers, intercessions, and thanksgivings be made for all men, [2]for kings and all who are in high positions, that we may lead a quiet and peaceable life, godly and respectful in every way. [3]This is good, and it is acceptable in the sight of God our Savior, [4]who desires all men to be saved and to come to the knowledge of the truth. [5]For there is one God, and there is one mediator between God

---

1:12–17 An autobiographical aside. Paul stands as a living exemplar of Christ's redemptive work, i.e., an example of how the Lord can transform even rebellious sinners into remarkable saints. In the end, the tragic tale of Saul the Pharisee became the epic story of Paul the Apostle because of one fact: the grace and mercy of God was poured out upon him (1:13; 1 Cor 15:10) (CCC 545).

1:15 foremost of sinners: The grace given to Paul at his conversion magnified his awareness of past faults. The comment is suggestive of the letter's authenticity, since it is unlikely that an admirer of Paul would describe him in more humiliating terms than the apostle himself did (1 Cor 15:9). See introduction: *Author.*

1:17 To the King of ages: Possibly a Jewish doxology that passed into the liturgy of the ancient Church. Others like it punctuate the letters of Paul (6:15–16; Rom 16:27; Phil 4:20; Eph 3:21).

1:18 prophetic utterances: This may indicate that Timothy's ordination was accompanied by a revelation of his precise mission to the Ephesian Church (4:14). A similar missionary calling is outlined in Acts 13:1–3.

1:20 Hymenaeus and Alexander: Ringleaders of the erring teachers in Ephesus. So dangerous was their teaching that Paul surrendered them to **Satan**, i.e., he excommunicated them from the life and liturgy of the Church. This drastic measure is not an irreversible condemnation but a form of disciplinary correction designed to bring about their repentance. Nothing more is known of them unless Hymenaeus is the same person mentioned in 2 Tim 2:17 and unless this Alexander can be linked with the individual in Acts 19:33 or 2 Tim 4:14–15. See note on 1 Cor 5:5.

2:1–15 The entire chapter is devoted to prayer, the first half concerning intercessory prayer for ecclesiastical and government leaders (2:1–7), and the second with liturgical prayers offered by men and women (2:8–15). Timothy's task is to reorder public worship in Ephesus according to Paul's directives.

2:2 kings . . . high positions: Prayer for civic officials is a continuation of the Jewish custom to offer prayers and sacrifices for secular rulers (Ezra 6:10; 1 Mac 7:33; CCC 1900).

2:4 desires all men to be saved: The Father wants all to repent and receive the salvation offered by Christ (4:10; 2 Pet 3:9). It is wrong, therefore, to contend that Jesus died to redeem only select individuals and not the human family as a whole (1 Jn 2:2). Believers act on this conviction when they intercede for the temporal and spiritual needs of "all men" (2:1)

(CCC 851, 1821). **knowledge of the truth:** A summary of this knowledge is formulated in the very next sentence (2:5–6), where saving truth is linked with the substance of the gospel (Gal 2:5; Col 1:5).

2:5 one God: The monotheistic faith of Israel (Deut 6:4), which remains a standing truth of the gospel (Jn 17:3; 1 Cor 8:6) (CCC 200–202). **one mediator:** A middleman or negotiator who makes friends of enemies. Jesus Christ is the mediator who reconciles the world to the Father in the bonds of the New Covenant (2 Cor 5:18; Heb 9:15). The distance once separating man from God is now bridged by the Incarnation, in which divinity and humanity are forever united in God the Son. In this sense, the mediation of Christ is absolutely unique. Still, the mediation of angels and saints is not ruled out, since union with Christ enables others to share in the saving work of Christ in subordinate and participatory ways. Paul assumes as much in the immediate context, for he urges Timothy

---

Word Study

Conscience (1 Tim 1:19)

Syneidēsis (Gk): "moral consciousness". The term is used six times in the Pastoral Epistles and 24 times in the rest of the NT. It refers to a hidden law in the heart that obliges us to do good and avoid evil (Rom 2:15). As an interior judge, it either approves our actions as praiseworthy (2 Cor 1:12) or accuses us of sins committed (Wis 17:11). Habitual sin can cause the voice of conscience to be muffled over time, making sinners responsible for their own inability to distinguish right from wrong (Tit 1:15). Conversely, to serve God with a good or clear conscience is to listen to its guidance and act in accord with its directives (Acts 24:16; Heb 13:18). Baptism plays an important part in this, as it gives us a new start by cleansing our conscience of past failures (Heb 10:22; 1 Pet 3:21). For Paul, our concern for conscience must also extend to our neighbor. He warns that when Christians act irresponsibly, they can cause the consciences of weaker believers to be wounded (1 Cor 8:12; 10:27–29) (CCC 1776–89).

---

[b] Greek *to the ages of ages.*

and men, the man Christ Jesus, [6]who gave himself as a ransom for all, the testimony to which was given at the proper time. [7]For this I was appointed a preacher and apostle (I am telling the truth, I am not lying), a teacher of the Gentiles in faith and truth.

8 I desire then that in every place the men should pray, lifting holy hands without anger or quarreling; [9]also that women should adorn themselves modestly and sensibly in seemly apparel, not with braided hair or gold or pearls or costly attire [10]but by good deeds, as befits women who profess religion. [11]Let a woman learn in silence with all submissiveness. [12]I permit no woman to teach or to have authority over men; she is to keep silent. [13]For Adam was formed first, then Eve;

[14]and Adam was not deceived, but the woman was deceived and became a transgressor. [15]Yet woman will be saved through bearing children, [c] if she continues [d] in faith and love and holiness, with modesty.

Qualifications of Bishops

3 The saying is sure: If any one aspires to the office of bishop, he desires a noble task. [2]Now a bishop must be above reproach, the husband of one wife, temperate, sensible, dignified, hospitable, an apt teacher, [3]no drunkard, not violent but gentle, not quarrelsome, and no lover of money. [4]He must manage his own household well, keeping his children submissive and respectful in every way; [5]for if a man does not know how to manage his own household, how can he care for

---

2:13: Gen 2:7, 21–22.   **2:14:** Gen 3:1–6.

---

and company to *pray* for civil authorities, i.e., to intercede as mediators between God and their governors in the course of the liturgy (2:1–3) (CCC 618, 970, 1349, 2636). ● A mediator brings together those who are separated, for extremes are united at a midpoint. Uniting men with God is the office of Christ, through whom men are reconciled to God. However, nothing forbids others from being called mediators inasmuch as they cooperate in uniting men with God by directing their way or by ministerial actions (St. Thomas Aquinas, *Summa Theologiae* III, 26, 1).

2:6 gave himself: The Crucifixion of Jesus was a voluntary act of sacrifice and thus a death he freely accepted (Eph 5:2). **ransom:** A price paid for the release of captives. See word study: *Ransom* at Mk 10.

2:8 lifting holy hands: Raising the hands in prayer was a revered custom in ancient Israel (Ps 141:2; Is 1:15). Artwork discovered in the Roman catacombs indicates that this practice continued into the early centuries of the Church. By calling the hands "holy", Paul is saying that reverent posture must be coupled with an inward desire for personal holiness. **without anger:** Peace between believers makes worship acceptable to the Lord (Mt 5:23–24). Sin and strife can thwart the effectiveness of our prayers (Ps 66:18; 1 Pet 3:7).

2:9 modestly and sensibly: Decorum guidelines for the liturgy. Female attire should be modest, not overrevealing or fitted to arouse the base passions of men in attendance. It should also be sensible, not a vain display of fashion, wealth, or social status, which are ultimately unimportant in God's eyes. Dressing for worship demands consideration for others as well as a humble reverence for the Lord. Similar instructions are given in 1 Pet 3:3–4 (CCC 2521–24).

2:12–16 Paul's teaching on women and gender roles has its basis in Genesis 2–3. ● The creation of Adam **first** appears in Gen 2:7, and **then** Eve is formed in Gen 2:21–22. Mention that Eve was **deceived** is a reference to her words in Gen 3:13. Also, the subordination of woman to the **authority** of man, along with her difficult task of **bearing children**, recalls the penitential curse laid upon Eve in Gen 3:16. Note that Paul is not attempting to downplay the sin of Adam by shifting attention to Eve; he is fully aware of the disaster caused by the rebellion of the first man (Rom 5:12–21; 1 Cor 15:22).

2:12 I permit no woman to teach: Not an absolute prohibition that applies to all circumstances, but one that excludes women from the teaching ministry exercised by ordained clergymen (1 Cor 14:34–35). Paul is not denying the equal dignity of men and women in Christ (Gal 3:28) or the

propriety of women in praying and prophesying within the context of worship (1 Cor 11:5). Women perform an invaluable service when they teach the faith in other contexts by their words and Christian example (Tit 2:3–4). ● According to Church teaching, Paul forbids women to exercise the official function of teaching in the Christian assembly (Sacred Congregation for the Doctrine of the Faith, *Inter insigniores* [1976], 4).

2:15 bearing children: Motherhood can be a means of sanctification and salvation, provided the woman exemplifies feminine virtues. Emphasis on the dignity of motherhood may be aimed at certain teachers who denied the goodness of marriage (4:3) or at women who found masculine roles more appealing (2:12). Notice that marriage and child rearing are not the only paths open to women, for Paul also extols the excellence of the single life (1 Cor 7:25–35) (CCC 1652–53).

3:1–13 Paul turns to the topic of Christian leadership, considering bishops (3:1–7) as well as deacons and deaconesses (3:8–13). He outlines not their duties so much as the human virtues expected of them, such as integrity, sobriety, and respectability. Timothy must take this to heart as he selects and ordains worthy candidates for these positions (5:22).

3:1 bishop: An overseer or spiritual shepherd who carries on the mission of the original apostles. Note that the titles "bishop" and "elder/presbyter" were somewhat fluid in the earliest years of the Church, and it seems that they could be used interchangeably (Acts 20:17, 28; Tit 1:5–7). Soon, however, the distinction between bishops (3:1), elders (5:17), and deacons (3:8) was clearly defined and their respective titles standardized. ● As if to say that the traditions of the apostles were taken from the Old Testament, bishops, presbyters, and deacons occupy in the Church the same positions that Aaron, his sons, and the Levites occupied in the Temple (St. Jerome, *Letters* 146). ● The Church recognizes these offices as three degrees of the Sacrament of Holy Orders: the episcopate (bishops), the presbyterate (elders or priests), and the diaconate (deacons) (CCC 1554–71).

3:2 one wife: Candidates for pastoral ministry should not be married more than once in their lifetime (3:12). Paul does not specify why, but his teaching elsewhere suggests (1) that widowers who remain unmarried will be better able to devote themselves to the Lord's work (1 Cor 7:8, 32–34) and (2) that widowers who pursue remarriage may be lacking the self-control expected of a minister of the gospel (1 Cor 7:9, 36–38). On the question of clerical celibacy, see note on 1 Cor 9:5 (CCC 1579–80).

3:5 his own household: The assumption is that bishops are spiritual fathers. Failure to supervise well the affairs of their own families and households suggests they will lack the necessary virtues to shepherd the household of God, which is the Church (3:15; Gal 6:10).

---

[c] Or *by the birth of the child.*
[d] Greek *they continue.*

God's Church? [6]He must not be a recent convert, or he may be puffed up with conceit and fall into the condemnation of the devil; [f] [7]moreover he must be well thought of by outsiders, or he may fall into reproach and the snare of the devil. [f]

Qualifications of Deacons

8 Deacons likewise must be serious, not double-tongued, not addicted to much wine, not greedy for gain; [9]they must hold the mystery of the faith with a clear conscience. [10]And let them also be tested first; then if they prove themselves blameless let them serve as deacons. [11]The women likewise must be serious, no slanderers, but temperate, faithful in all things. [12]Let deacons be the husband of one wife, and let them manage their children and their households well; [13]for those who serve well as deacons gain a good standing for themselves and also great confidence in the faith which is in Christ Jesus.

The Mystery of Our Religion

14 I hope to come to you soon, but I am writing these instructions to you so that, [15]if I am delayed, you may know how one ought to behave in the household of God, which is the Church of the living God, the pillar and bulwark of the truth. [16]Great indeed, we confess, is the mystery of our religion:

He [h] was manifested in the flesh,
vindicated [i] in the Spirit,
    seen by angels,
preached among the nations,
believed on in the world,
    taken up in glory.

False Asceticism

4 Now the Spirit expressly says that in later times some will depart from the faith by giving heed to deceitful spirits and doctrines of demons, [2]through the pretensions of liars whose consciences are seared, [3]who forbid marriage and enjoin absti-

---

3:8 Deacons: Ministers who assist the bishops (Phil 1:1) and serve the needs of the poor, sick, and widowed. They probably had limited liturgical responsibilities as well. The beginning of this office is sometimes traced to the seven men ordained for service in Acts 6:1–6. See note on Acts 6:6 (CCC 1569–70).

3:9 mystery of the faith: The full range of revealed truths given through Christ. Paul regularly connects this with the Father's overarching plan to bring all nations into the kingdom of God (Rom 16:25–26; Eph 1:9–10). See word study: *Mystery* at Eph 3:3.

3:11 women likewise: Either a reference to the wives of the deacons (3:8) or to deaconesses, who assisted with the catechetical instruction and Baptism of women (Rom 16:1).
• The Church recognizes that deaconesses were *appointed* for special tasks but not *ordained* for sacramental ministry in the strict sense. The First Council of Nicaea decreed in A.D. 325 that women deacons are numbered among the laity and not among the ordained clergy (Canon 19) (CCC 1577).

3:14 I am writing: Paul intends to rejoin Timothy in Ephesus at his earliest convenience (1:3).

3:15 pillar and bulwark: The terms refer to structural supports that hold up a building. The Church is set in place to support the edifice of gospel truth. The Spirit makes this possible by enabling the successors of the apostles to preserve the apostolic faith from corruption and distortion as the centuries pass. Without this protective grace, the bishops of the Church would be no more than fallible human teachers unequipped to fulfill the mission granted to them by the Lord. Other passages suggest that Paul may envision the leaders of the Church as the pillars and foundation stones of God's living Temple (Gal 2:9; Eph 2:20; CCC 171, 768, 2032). See note on Jn 16:13.

3:16 He was manifested: Several features in the Greek text suggest Paul is quoting from an ancient Christian hymn. It touches on key moments in the incarnate life of Christ: his coming as a man (**manifested**), his Resurrection (**vindicated**), his adoration in heaven (**seen by angels**), the spread of his message (**preached**), its acceptance in the world (**believed on**), and his Ascension into glory (**taken up**) (CCC 463, 2641).

4:1 in later times: Applies not only to the closing days of history, but also to the present age of the New Covenant, which for Paul already stands at the "end of the ages" (1 Cor 10:11). The explosion of error and confusion expected in these days is likewise mentioned in 2 Pet 3:3 and Jude 18 (CCC 672).

4:3 forbid marriage: Timothy is put on guard against teachers who deny the goodness of marriage. Even Paul, who actively promotes celibacy (1 Cor 7:25–26), firmly upholds the

---

[f] Or *slanderer*.
[h] Greek *Who*; other ancient authorities read *God*; others, *Which*.
[i] Or *justified*.

The Threefold Pastoral Ministry

Scripture tells us that Jesus Christ transformed and fulfilled the institutions of the Old Covenant once entrusted to Israel. The hierarchy of covenant leadership is no exception to this rule. Yahweh established three tiers of Levitical ministry to lead the sacrificial worship of the Temple, and later three levels of leadership were established in the Jewish synagogue to preach the Scriptures and serve the community of faith. The liturgies that revolved around sacrifice (Temple) and Scripture (synagogue) were eventually brought together in Christian worship, where the Word is proclaimed and the Sacraments are administered. For good reason, then, the three-tiered leadership of the Temple and synagogue was a fitting model for the threefold structure of the Church's own pastoral ministry, established to lead, teach, and sanctify the People of God.

Temple	Synagogue	Church
High Priest	Ruler of Synagogue	Bishop
Priests	Board of Elders	Presbyters (Priests)
Levites	Servants	Deacons

nence from foods which God created to be received with thanksgiving by those who believe and know the truth. ⁴For everything created by God is good, and nothing is to be rejected if it is received with thanksgiving; ⁵for then it is consecrated by the word of God and prayer.

A Good Minister of Jesus Christ

6 If you put these instructions before the brethren, you will be a good minister of Christ Jesus, nourished on the words of the faith and of the good doctrine which you have followed. ⁷Have nothing to do with godless and silly myths. Train yourself in godliness; ⁸for while bodily training is of some value, godliness is of value in every way, as it holds promise for the present life and also for the life to come. ⁹The saying is sure and worthy of full acceptance. ¹⁰For to this end we toil and strive, ʲ because we have our hope set on the living God, who is the Savior of all men, especially of those who believe.

11 Command and teach these things. ¹²Let no one despise your youth, but set the believers an example in speech and conduct, in love, in faith, in purity. ¹³Till I come, attend to the public reading of Scripture, to preaching, to teaching. ¹⁴Do not neglect the gift you have, which was given you by

prophetic utterance when the elders laid their hands upon you. ¹⁵Practice these duties, devote yourself to them, so that all may see your progress. ¹⁶Take heed to yourself and to your teaching; hold to that, for by so doing you will save both yourself and your hearers.

Duties toward Believers

5 Do not rebuke an older man but exhort him as you would a father; treat younger men like brothers, ²older women like mothers, younger women like sisters, in all purity.

3 Honor widows who are real widows. ⁴If a widow has children or grandchildren, let them first learn their religious duty to their own family and make some return to their parents; for this is acceptable in the sight of God. ⁵She who is a real widow, and is left all alone, has set her hope on God and continues in supplications and prayers night and day; ⁶whereas she who is self-indulgent is dead even while she lives. ⁷Command this, so that they may be without reproach. ⁸If any one does not provide for his relatives, and especially for his own family, he has disowned the faith and is worse than an unbeliever.

9 Let a widow be enrolled if she is not less than sixty years of age, having been the wife of one

---

propriety and sanctity of married life (Eph 5:21–33). See note on 1 Cor 7:1. **abstinence from foods:** Possibly a reference to the dietary restrictions of the Old Covenant (Lev 11). The warning is issued because these laws are no longer binding upon believers in the New Covenant (Mk 7:18–19; Acts 10:9–16). Some suggest this twofold ban on marriage and certain foods reflects an incipient form of Gnosticism, a second-century heresy that saw the material world as evil and called adherents to rise above the demands of their physical life as far as possible. Timothy is cautioned, not against asceticism itself, but against deviant forms of it that develop when the goodness of creation is denied (4:4; Gen 1:31).

4:5 consecrated by . . . prayer: Mealtime prayers are a regular feature of both Jewish and Christian tradition.

4:7 silly myths: Useless speculation about OT figures. See note on 1:4.

4:8 bodily training: Spiritual wellness is more important than bodily health. Nevertheless, the training regiment of athletes is a fitting model for the discipline and commitment necessary to advance in the spiritual life. See note on 1 Cor 9:24–27.

4:10 Savior of all: Paul does not mean that everyone will escape damnation in the end. He is stressing that God's call to salvation is universal so that all who respond will find eternal life, regardless of their sex, age, language, or nationality (Acts 10:34–35; Gal 3:28; CCC 1058, 1261). See note on 1 Tim 2:4. ● Vatican II affirms the possibility that even those who know nothing of the gospel may be saved by the grace of Christ, provided they seek God sincerely, follow the dictates of their conscience, and cooperate with the help given to them by divine Providence (*Lumen Gentium* 16).

4:12 your youth: There was a danger that young Timothy, probably in his thirties, would be intimidated or not held in respect by the elders of the Ephesian Church he was sent to correct (5:20). He is reminded that his reform efforts will succeed only if he practices the charity he preaches.

4:13 reading of Scripture: One of the earliest references to the recitation of Scripture in the course of the liturgy (1 Thess

5:27; Rev 1:3). This practice passed into the ancient Church from the synagogue (Lk 4:16; Acts 15:21).

4:14 the elders: Includes Paul, along with the assembled bishops of the Ephesian Church (2 Tim 1:6). **laid their hands upon:** The imposition of hands is a gesture with various meanings in the Bible. It was done to (1) perform healings (Mk 16:18), (2) confer blessings (Mt 19:13), (3) appoint missionaries (Acts 13:1–3), (4) bestow the Spirit on believers (Acts 8:17; 19:6), (5) unload the sins of Israel onto sacrificial beasts (Lev 16:21), (6) transfer religious authority from one leader to another (Num 27:18–23; Deut 34:9), and (7) appoint the Levites for sacred ministry (Num 8:10–11). ● These last two examples (6 and 7) provide the immediate background for the New Covenant rite of priestly ordination. Timothy's consecration as a bishop gives him the fullness of priestly and apostolic authority to ordain others as well (5:22). Jewish rabbis were similarly appointed by a council of synagogue elders who laid hands on the candidate (CCC 1573–76).

5:1—6:2 Paul instructs Timothy on how to treat older and younger believers (5:1–2), widows (5:3–16), elders (5:17–25), and slaves (6:1–2). He leads in with a reminder that every Christian under his care is a member of the spiritual family of Christ (5:1–2).

5:3–16 Widows had special needs in ancient society, where no economic or governmental programs were in place to assist them. Paul advises different support systems for different circumstances. **(1)** Widows with a surviving family should be cared for by their children and relatives (5:4). **(2)** Older widows without family or wealth are to receive material support from the local church (5:16). **(3)** Younger widows are advised to remarry, lest their energies and idle time be spent in unwholesome conduct and conversation (5:14).

5:5 prayers night and day: A good example is the aged widow Anna in Lk 2:37.

5:6 dead: Spiritually lifeless (Eph 2:1; Rev 3:1).

5:9 enrolled: Either added to a list of widows who qualify to receive assistance or registered among an organized group of widows committed to prayer (5:5) and works of service (5:10). The character expected of these women is comparable to that of a prospective bishop (3:2) or deacon (3:8).

ʲ Other ancient authorities read *suffer reproach.*

husband; [10]and she must be well attested for her good deeds, as one who has brought up children, shown hospitality, washed the feet of the saints, relieved the afflicted, and devoted herself to doing good in every way. [11]But refuse to enrol younger widows; for when they grow wanton against Christ they desire to marry, [12]and so they incur condemnation for having violated their first pledge. [13]Besides that, they learn to be idlers, gadding about from house to house, and not only idlers but gossips and busybodies, saying what they should not. [14]So I would have younger widows marry, bear children, rule their households, and give the enemy no occasion to revile us. [15]For some have already strayed after Satan. [16]If any believing woman [1] has relatives who are widows, let her assist them; let the Church not be burdened, so that it may assist those who are real widows.

17 Let the elders who rule well be considered worthy of double honor, especially those who labor in preaching and teaching; [18]for the Scripture says, "You shall not muzzle an ox when it is treading out the grain," and, "The laborer deserves his wages." [19]Never admit any charge against an elder except on the evidence of two or three witnesses. [20]As for those who persist in sin, rebuke them in the presence of all, so that the rest may stand in fear. [21]In the presence of God and of Christ Jesus and of the elect angels I charge you to keep these rules without favor, doing nothing from partiality. [22]Do not be hasty in the laying on of hands, nor participate in another man's sins; keep yourself pure.

23 No longer drink only water, but use a little wine for the sake of your stomach and your frequent ailments.

Men's Deeds, False Teaching, and True Riches

24 The sins of some men are conspicuous, pointing to judgment, but the sins of others appear later. [25]So also good deeds are conspicuous; and even when they are not, they cannot remain hidden.

6 Let all who are under the yoke of slavery regard their masters as worthy of all honor, so that the name of God and the teaching may not be defamed. [2]Those who have believing masters must not be disrespectful on the ground that they are brethren; rather they must serve all the better since those who benefit by their service are believers and beloved.

Teach and urge these duties. [3]If any one teaches otherwise and does not agree with the sound words of our Lord Jesus Christ and the teaching which accords with godliness, [4]he is puffed up with conceit, he knows nothing; he has a morbid craving for controversy and for disputes about words, which produce envy, dissension, slander, base suspicions, [5]and wrangling among men who are depraved in mind and bereft of the truth, imagining that godliness is a means of gain. [6]There is great gain in godliness with contentment; [7]for we brought nothing into the world, and [m] we cannot take anything out of the world; [8]but if we have food and clothing, with these we shall be content. [9]But those who desire to be rich fall into temptation, into a snare, into many senseless and hurtful desires that plunge men into ruin and destruction. [10]For the love of money is the root of all evils; it is through this craving that some have wandered away from the faith and pierced their hearts with many pangs.

5:18: Deut 25:4; 1 Cor 9:9; Mt 10:10; Lk 10:7; 1 Cor 9:14.   **5:19:** Deut 19:15.

5:10 washed the feet: An act of hospitality common in societies where sandals are worn and dusty roads are traveled on foot (Lk 7:44). Jesus made it a symbol of Christian service (Jn 13:14–17).

5:17 the elders: Or "presbyters" (priests). Being servants of the gospel, they deserve our highest respect as well as a share of our material resources. Only in extreme cases where sin is at issue should Timothy rebuke an elder in public (5:20). See chart: *The Threefold Pastoral Ministry* at 1 Tim 3.

5:18 Scripture says: By the time Paul wrote 1 Timothy, certain books of the NT were apparently being revered as part of holy Scripture. In this passage, Paul seems to assume that the citations from Deuteronomy and the Gospel of Luke share the same authority as inspired writings. Some of his own letters were esteemed in this way as well (2 Pet 3:15–16). **You shall not muzzle:** A quotation of Deut 25:4. For Paul, permitting animals to eat while they work carries a hidden significance now revealed by the gospel, so that what is true for oxen is even truer for ordained elders: their work entitles them to a share in the community's food and provisions (1 Cor 9:9–10). The allegorical meaning of this OT passage corresponds to the literal meaning of the NT passage that follows. **laborer deserves his wages:** A verbatim quotation of Lk 10:7, where Jesus in-

sists that ministers of the Word have a right to fair compensation for their preaching (CCC 2122). See note on Lk 10:7.

5:19 two or three witnesses: Judicial criteria in a Jewish court of law (Deut 19:15). See note on 2 Cor 13:1.

5:22 Do not be hasty: Timothy is told to screen candidates for pastoral ministry before ordaining them by the sacramental imposition of hands. Otherwise, the hurried promotion of immature or poorly formed believers might have ruinous consequences (3:6). See note on 1 Tim 4:14.

5:23 your frequent ailments: Timothy's fragile health was a concern to Paul. He is advised to consume wine in moderation and so benefit from its medicinal properties. Wine can sometimes offset the uncomfortable effects of drinking impure water. See note on Eph 5:18.

6:1 slavery: The conversion of slaves and their masters in the early Church raised questions of how these relationships should be handled by believers (Col 3:22–4:1). Paul insists that slaves must honor their masters and that masters must respect their slaves, lest Christians acquire a reputation for being either insubordinate or inhumane. Without approving the institution of slavery as such, he is stressing that every station in life provides opportunities to serve the Lord. See note on Eph 6:5.

6:3–10 Paul resumes his criticism of false teachers wreaking havoc in Ephesus (1:3–11). He contends that the driving force behind their novelties is pride, an infatuation with controversy,

---

[1] Other ancient authorities read *man or woman*; others, simply *man*

[m] Other ancient authorities insert *it is certain that.*

The Good Fight of Faith

11 But as for you, man of God, shun all this; aim at righteousness, godliness, faith, love, steadfastness, gentleness. [12]Fight the good fight of the faith; take hold of the eternal life to which you were called when you made the good confession in the presence of many witnesses. [13]In the presence of God who gives life to all things, and of Christ Jesus who in his testimony before Pontius Pilate made the good confession, [14]I charge you to keep the commandment unstained and free from reproach until the appearing of our Lord Jesus Christ; [15]and this will be made manifest at the proper time by the blessed and only Sovereign, the King of kings and Lord of lords, [16]who alone has immortality and dwells in unapproachable light, whom no man has ever seen or can see. To him be honor and eternal dominion. Amen.

17 As for the rich in this world, charge them not to be haughty, nor to set their hopes on uncertain riches but on God who richly furnishes us with everything to enjoy. [18]They are to do good, to be rich in good deeds, liberal and generous, [19]thus laying up for themselves a good foundation for the future, so that they may take hold of the life which is life indeed.

Personal Instructions and Benediction

20 O Timothy, guard what has been entrusted to you. Avoid the godless chatter and contradictions of what is falsely called knowledge, [21]for by professing it some have missed the mark as regards the faith.

Grace be with you.

6:13: Jn 18:37.

---

and a distorted view of leadership. Not only that, but they exact a price for their preaching in order to accumulate wealth for themselves (6:10; Tit 1:11).

6:7 nothing into the world: Recalls similar statements in Job 1:21 and Eccles 5:15.

✠ **6:10 the love of money:** Paul reproves, not the wealthy, but lovers of wealth. So dangerous is the allurement of riches that he warns in the strongest possible terms against piling it up for ourselves. Unless we become "poor in spirit" (Mt 5:3), the downward pull of money and material possessions will eventually lead to destruction (Lk 12:15–21). • What evils are caused by wealth! There are frauds, robberies, miseries, enmities, contentions, battles. Take away the love of money, and you put an end to war, conflict, enmity, strife, and contention (St. John Chrysostom, *Homilies on 1 Timothy* 17).

6:12 the good confession: Probably Timothy's profession of faith enunciated at his Baptism. Paul is urging him to live out his baptismal promises to the full (CCC 2145).

6:13 before Pontius Pilate: Refers to Jesus' testimony to the truth at his trial before the governor (Mk 15:1–2; Jn 18:33–37).

6:14 the appearing: The visible manifestation of Christ at his Second Coming (1 Thess 4:16; Tit 2:13).

6:15 King of kings . . . Lord of lords: A reference to God's superiority over every earthly ruler (Ps 136:2–3; Dan 2:47; 2

Mac 13:4). These titles are applied directly to Christ in Rev 17:14 and 19:16.

✠ **6:20 O Timothy, guard:** The faith that Timothy holds and teaches is a sacred trust given to him for safekeeping (2 Tim 1:14; 2:2; Jude 3). The duty to preserve it intact is all the more important in places such as Ephesus, where counterfeit doctrines are vying for the hearts and minds of local believers (1:3–7) (CCC 84). • What is entrusted to you is not what you have discovered. It is what you have received, not what you have thought up for yourself. It is a matter, not of ingenuity, but of doctrine; not of personal opinion, but of public tradition. You are not the author, but the guardian. So preserve inviolate and undamaged the trust of the Catholic faith (St. Vincent of Lérins, *The Commonitory* 22). **falsely called knowledge:** The perverted teachings of the Ephesian troublemakers. Interpreters have often taken this to mean that the false teachers are Gnostics, i.e., proponents of a second-century religious system that viewed the possession of "secret knowledge" as a pathway to salvation. This verse alone cannot support the conclusion, but see note on 1 Tim 4:3.

6:21 Grace be with you: Since the best Greek manuscripts have "you" in the plural, many have reasoned that the letter, while primarily sent to Timothy, was also intended to be read before the Ephesian congregation.

STUDY QUESTIONS
1 Timothy

Chapter 1

For understanding
1. **1:2.** Who was Timothy, and what was his relationship with Paul? What does the expression "my true child" imply about Paul's attitude toward his ministry? How does Timothy figure into that attitude?
2. **1:8.** Why is the Law or Torah "good"? How does Paul indicate that the moral precepts of the Old Covenant are carried over into the New Covenant? What does the term "lawfully" mean here? If the purpose of the Torah is not to encourage useless conjectures and confusion, what is its purpose?
3. **Word Study: Conscience (1:19).** What does the Greek word for *conscience* mean? What does it oblige us to do and to avoid? How does it act as an interior judge? What are the effects on conscience of habitual sin? Conversely, what are the effects of a good and clear conscience? For Paul, to whom does our concern for conscience extend, and why?
4. **1:20.** Who were Hymenaeus and Alexander, and what became of them? Since excommunication is a drastic measure, what was Paul's purpose in applying it to them?

For application
1. **1:5.** What is the aim of Paul's charge to Timothy about his teaching, and from what three things does it come? Why are these things important when giving doctrinal instruction?
2. **1:8–11.** For whom are the moral prescriptions of the Law laid down, according to these verses? Even though many commands of the law are phrased in the negative ("You shall not . . ."), what is their positive value for those who obey them? For example, what is the positive value in obeying commands to avoid the types of offenses that Paul lists?
3. **1:12–16.** Of what value to others' faith are the stories of notorious criminals or sinners who have been converted and are now living exemplary lives? What has been your own experience with the mercy of conversion?
4. **1:18–19.** From the viewpoint of faith, why is it better to live a good life than a wicked one? What do you think of the opinion, sometimes expressed by celebrities and pundits, that people who flout the moral law are "more interesting" than those who keep it? In a world like ours, how is living according to a clean conscience more interesting than habitually violating it?

Chapter 2

For understanding
1. **2:1–15.** To what is this entire chapter devoted? How is it divided? What is Timothy's task?
2. **2:5.** What is a *mediator*? As a mediator, what does Jesus Christ do? Since there is one mediator between God and man—Jesus Christ—how is the mediation of saints and angels possible? How does Paul encourage Timothy and company to act as mediators?
3. **2:12.** To what is Paul's prohibition of women as teachers restricted? What is Paul *not* denying about women? If women cannot act in an official capacity as ordained preachers and homilists, according to Paul, in what capacity can they serve as teachers?
4. **2:12–16.** What is the background for Paul's teaching on gender roles? What specific passages does he have in mind? Does his focus on the deception of Eve imply that the sin of Adam is unimportant? How would you support your answer?

For application
1. **2:1–2.** For whom do you regularly intercede in prayer? For whom should you intercede regularly but do not right now? When you do intercede, for what do you pray?
2. **2:8.** Do you ever pray in a group with others (outside of the liturgy)? What are some of the benefits of group prayer?

3. **2:9–10.** Why would Paul insist on modesty in dress and personal accessories? How do you dress when you attend Sunday Mass?
4. **2:15.** How can being a parent promote one's salvation? What virtues does parenthood tend to generate or encourage?

Chapter 3

For understanding
1. **3:1.** What is the role of the bishop? How were the titles of "bishop" and "elder/presbyter" understood in the earliest years of the Church? How does the Church recognize these offices now?
2. **Chart: The Threefold Pastoral Ministry.** In the Old Covenant, how many tiers of pastoral ministry were there—and what were they? What were they when translated from Temple (sacrifice) to the synagogue (Scripture)? What happens in Christian worship that makes these Old Covenant offices a good model for us?
3. **3:11.** Suppose for a moment this verse refers to deaconesses. What, most likely, was their role? How were they set apart for that role? What did the first Council of Nicaea (A.D. 325) conclude about their status? What does CCC 1577 say with respect to ordination?
4. **3:15.** Why is the Church called the "pillar and bulwark" of the truth? How does the Holy Spirit make this possible? How might Paul be thinking of the apostolic leaders of the Church?

For application
1. **3:1–5.** If you are married, how do these verses apply to the way you manage your own household? Whether you are married or not, how do they apply to the way you manage your social relationships?
2. **3:6.** Why would Paul advise against recent converts from paganism becoming teachers of the faith? Given the zeal of those who come into full communion with the Catholic Church from non-Catholic Christian traditions, might the same caution apply to them?
3. **3:8–11.** How might these verses, which are directed to deacons, also apply to you? What does verse 9 teach us about dissent from Catholic moral teaching?
4. **3:13.** How might deacons and other pastoral ministers "gain . . . great confidence in the faith" through their ministry?

Chapter 4

For understanding
1. **4:3.** Why would Gnosticism forbid marriage and enjoin against certain foods? What did Gnosticism call its adherents to rise above? If Paul is not cautioning Timothy against asceticism, what is he cautioning him against?
2. **4:13.** To what practice is this verse one of the earliest references? Where did Christians get the practice?
3. **4:14.** In the Bible, what meanings does the gesture of the "imposition of hands" have? Which two meanings from the OT are connected to what Paul describes here? What does Timothy's consecration as a bishop give him? How were Jewish rabbis appointed?

For application
1. **4:1–3.** How do you as an adult Catholic form your conscience in accord with the truth, so that it is not likely to be victimized by false teaching or "seared" by sinful choices?
2. **4:7–8.** What ways do you have of "training yourself spiritually"? What kinds of spiritual reading do you do? Where do you go for spiritual counsel? What kinds of self-discipline do you practice?
3. **4:13.** How attentive are you to the reading of Scripture in the liturgy? What practices do you follow for the private reading of Scripture?
4. **4:14.** Since everyone has some charism (gift given by the Holy Spirit) to share with others, what gift(s) do you have? How do you nourish what God has given you to share? If you are ordained or appointed to some kind of ministry, how would you apply Paul's advice not to neglect it?

Chapter 5

For understanding
1. **5:3–16.** Why was Paul so concerned about widows? What kinds of support systems does he advise in these verses?
2. **5:9.** Into what kinds of groups could widows be "enrolled"? In what way do you think the character of enrolled widows might be comparable to that of bishops and deacons?
3. **5:18.** In Paul's day, how were some books of the NT being regarded as compared with those of the OT? What is an example of one of these NT books? Which passage from a NT book is Paul quoting verbatim?
4. **5:23.** Why does Paul recommend that Timothy drink a moderate amount of wine? What effects can it sometimes counteract?

For application
1. **5:1–2.** How does Paul advise you to treat an older man (unrelated to you) with whom you have a disagreement? How should you relate to members of the opposite sex, regardless of their age?
2. **5:4–8.** Have you ever had occasion to fulfill your duty to care for an aged or infirm relative, especially a widowed parent? What were some of the spiritual benefits of this experience? How might such a responsibility bring you closer to God?
3. **5:13.** Gossip has traditionally been regarded as a social problem, sometimes seriously sinful. Why might that be? Have you ever engaged in gossip (regardless of what you call it)? Whom have you hurt as a result? What might you do to improve this area of your spiritual life?
4. **5:24–25.** Do you tend to see the dark side of others first or their good side? How do you view yourself? Have you ever had the experience of finding that someone you disliked had done a good deed that was temporarily hidden and emerged only later?

Chapter 6

For understanding
1. **6:1.** What problems did the conversion of slaves and their masters pose for the early Church? On what does Paul insist? Without explicitly approving of slavery, what does he stress?
2. **6:10.** What is Paul reproving? What danger does he see in it?
3. **6:20.** Why was the guarding of the faith so important in places such as Ephesus? Who are the persons promoting what Paul calls "false knowledge", according to many interpreters?
4. **6:21.** Why do many think that this letter was intended to be read before the entire Ephesian congregation, even though it is addressed to Timothy personally?

For application
1. **6:1.** If you are an employee under supervision, how do you show respect to your supervisor? What motives do you have for this respect? How should a Christian employee relate to an employer? If you are an employer, manager, or supervisor, how do you show respect to your subordinates? What motives do you have for this attitude? What motives does Paul give for respect?
2. **6:7–11.** If you have one overarching ambition in life, how would you describe it? Is it closer to verse 10 or to verse 11? If the former, what attention would you pay Paul's advice to "shun all this"?
3. **6:17–19.** If you are financially well off, how do you use your wealth to "take hold of the life that is life indeed"? For example, do you take care to give financial support to the Church? What kinds of almsgiving do you practice? Where can you be more generous?

INTRODUCTION TO THE
SECOND LETTER OF SAINT PAUL TO TIMOTHY

Author This letter claims to be authored by the Apostle Paul (1:1), as do the other Pastoral Epistles, 1 Timothy and Titus (1 Tim 1:1; Tit 1:1). Orthodox Christianity accepted this claim from earliest times, and it was not until the nineteenth century that the apostolic authorship of these letters was seriously questioned. This modern surge of skepticism has gained ground ever since and continues to dominate the thinking of many biblical scholars today. Nevertheless, there are still those who insist that Paul himself is the author of all three Pastoral Epistles. Consideration of the internal evidence of these letters, balanced with the external testimony of tradition, supports their Pauline origin with a reasonable degree of certainty. For details, see introduction to 1 Timothy: *Author*.

Date Fixing a date for 2 Timothy must account for the historical circumstances described in the letter, namely, Paul's imprisonment (1:8) in the metropolis of Rome (1:17), along with his realization that death is imminent (4:6). The NT mentions one Roman imprisonment from A.D. 60 to 62, but it says nothing about what happened to Paul after this two-year detainment (Acts 28:16). Early tradition extends the story by claiming that Paul was released after this first imprisonment but was incarcerated again in Rome a few years later and martyred under Emperor Nero around A.D. 67 (Eusebius, *Ecclesiastical History* 2, 22). Scholars who accept the historicity of this second incarceration often view it as the context in which 2 Timothy was written, and this is most likely correct. Other defenders of Pauline authorship date 2 Timothy to the time of his first Roman imprisonment as recorded in the Book of Acts, presuming it ended with his execution rather than his release. Scholarship that attributes the letter to an unknown author writing in Paul's name usually dates the letter soon after the apostle's death (the late 60s) or near the end of the first century (in the 80s or 90s).

Purpose Paul writes this letter to encourage his younger colleague Timothy and to summon him to Rome. At this point, Timothy is still in Ephesus, where Paul has stationed him to help reform the local Church (1 Tim 1:3). Since problems once facing this congregation have steadily worsened, the apostle urges Timothy to fulfill his teaching mission with all the zeal and endurance he can muster (2:1–3; 4:2–5). Youthful and reserved by nature, Timothy must now be manly and strong in the grace of God (1:7; 2:1). Paul himself is learning that

loyalty is a rare commodity in times of distress. In fact, the earliest persecution of Christians in Rome (beginning in ca. A.D. 64) is so fierce that many of his companions have deserted him outright (1:15; 4:10–11). Abandoned and on trial for his life, the aged apostle wants a trusted companion like Timothy at his side (4:9, 21).

Themes and Characteristics In many ways, 2 Timothy reads like a last will and testament. It is a moving account of how Paul, like a runner crossing the finish line, has reached the end of his apostolic career, with only the crown of martyrdom awaiting him (4:6–8). Young Timothy, instructed by the apostle for more than 15 years, is now asked to take up the mantle of his mentor and continue his ministry of preaching. With death at his doorstep, Paul hurriedly sends a letter filled with fatherly wisdom and warnings to prepare Timothy for the struggles ahead.

Of particular concern for Paul is the transmission of sound doctrine (1:13–14; 4:2–3). The apostle assures Timothy that he will have to contend with new and novel teachings that spread confusion and erode the faith of otherwise strong believers. Timothy's mission is to guard the gospel (1:14) and to continue in earnest the responsible work of an evangelist (2:2; 4:2–3). The Ephesian congregation under Timothy's care has already faced controversies and quarrels (1 Tim 1:3–7), and the spread of falsehood has taken its toll on certain housewives (3:6–7) and others whom Paul mentions by name (2:17–18). So, too, as Christian persecutions begin to intensify and spread more widely in the Empire, Timothy is assured that suffering is inevitable for an outspoken defender of truth (2:3; 3:12). Nevertheless, Paul urges Timothy to find courage in the apostle's own endurance (3:10–14) and in the inspired Scriptures he has known since childhood (3:15–17). The time will come when Timothy, too, must pass the torch to others who will teach and defend the gospel for future generations (2:2).

In all of this, Paul gives a sense of what is most important in Christian ministry. The truth of the gospel was for him a sacred gift entrusted to the apostles and their successors by the Holy Spirit (1:14). It is therefore not to be tampered with or falsified by those whose ears cannot endure what is contrary to their personal liking (4:3). Paul himself has defended the Lord for years in the face of persecution (3:11) and is now ready to give his life for him who has empowered him to preach the Christian message (4:6, 17).

OUTLINE OF THE SECOND LETTER OF SAINT PAUL TO TIMOTHY

1. **Opening Address (1:1–2)**

2. **Perseverance in Suffering (1:3—2:13)**
    A. Thanksgiving (1:3–5)
    B. Admonitions for Timothy (1:6–14)
    C. Update on Paul (1:15–18)
    D. Personal Endurance (2:1–13)

3. **Perseverance in Sound Doctrine (2:14—4:8)**
    A. Responsible Preaching (2:14–26)
    B. Times of Distress (3:1–9)
    C. Following Paul and Scripture (3:10–17)
    D. The Mission of an Evangelist (4:1–8)

4. **Conclusion (4:9–22)**
    A. Final Instructions and Warnings (4:9–18)
    B. Greetings and Benediction (4:19–22)

THE SECOND LETTER OF SAINT PAUL TO
TIMOTHY

Salutation

1 Paul, an apostle of Christ Jesus by the will of God according to the promise of the life which is in Christ Jesus,

2 To Timothy, my beloved child:

Grace, mercy, and peace from God the Father and Christ Jesus our Lord.

Thanksgiving and Encouragement

3 I thank God whom I serve with a clear conscience, as did my fathers, when I remember you constantly in my prayers. ⁴As I remember your tears, I long night and day to see you, that I may be filled with joy. ⁵I am reminded of your sincere faith, a faith that dwelt first in your grandmother Lois and your mother Eunice and now, I am sure, dwells in you. ⁶For this reason I remind you to rekindle the gift of God that is within you through the laying on of my hands; ⁷for God did not give us a spirit of timidity but a spirit of power and love and self-control.

8 Do not be ashamed then of testifying to our Lord, nor of me his prisoner, but take your share of suffering for the gospel in the power of God, ⁹who saved us and called us with a holy calling, not in virtue of our works but in virtue of his own purpose and the grace which he gave us in Christ Jesus ages ago, ¹⁰and now has manifested through the appearing of our Savior Christ Jesus, who abolished death and brought life and immortality to light through the gospel. ¹¹For this gospel I was appointed a preacher and apostle and teacher, ¹²and therefore I suffer as I do. But I am not ashamed, for I know whom I have believed, and I am sure that he is able to guard until that Day what has been entrusted to me. ᵃ ¹³Follow the pattern of the sound words which you

---

1:5: Acts 16:1.

1:1 Paul, an apostle: The sender of the letter, not the addressee, is named first in ancient epistles. Paul was appointed an ambassador of Jesus Christ and commissioned to spread the gospel to Israel and all nations (1:11; Acts 9:15; 1 Cor 1:17). Paul's apostleship ranks him alongside the original Twelve selected by Jesus (Lk 6:13–16) (CCC 858). **promise of the life:** Eternal life, which we receive now as grace (1 Jn 5:13) and will possess more abundantly in the state of heavenly glory (Col 3:4; 1 Tim 4:8). Christ offers this life to the world through the preaching of the gospel and communicates it through the sacramental actions of the Church to those properly disposed to receive it (CCC 2, 1114–16).

1:2 Timothy: A friend and companion of Paul ever since his recruitment on the apostle's second missionary tour (Acts 16:1–3). See note on 1 Tim 1:2. **Grace, mercy, and peace:** A slight expansion of Paul's customary greeting of "grace" and "peace".

1:4 your tears: Probably shed at the last parting of Paul and Timothy in Ephesus (1 Tim 1:3). Since then, the apostle has not laid eyes on his coworker, despite intentions to rejoin him (1 Tim 3:14). This original plan probably fell through as a result of Paul's arrest and imprisonment (2:9).

1:5 your grandmother Lois: Otherwise unknown. **your mother Eunice:** A convert from Judaism who had instructed her son in the OT Scriptures since his childhood (3:15). Timothy's father was a Greek and may not have become a Christian (Acts 16:1). In any case, Paul is encouraged by the faith that Timothy inherited from the godly women of his family (CCC 2220).

🔔 **1:6 rekindle the gift:** Refers to the grace of priestly ministry. Timothy received the fullness of this grace when Paul and a gathering of elders ordained him as bishop by the imposition of hands (CCC 1558, 1577). He is now urged to make use of this divine help in order to complete his mission in Ephesus. See note on 1 Tim 4:14. ● Zeal is required to stir up the gift of God, for it lies within our power to kindle or quench this grace. By laziness and carelessness it is extinguished, and by attentiveness and diligence it is kept aflame (St. John Chrysostom, *Homilies on 2 Timothy* 1).

1:7 spirit of power Timothy is urged to yield himself to the supernatural strength of the Spirit, and this in order to be an effective teacher and shepherd.

1:8 his prisoner: Paul is nearly alone (4:10–11) and chained up like a criminal (2:9), suggesting this does not refer to his first Roman imprisonment, where he lived more comfortably under house arrest and was surrounded by friends and crowds eager to listen to him (Acts 28:16–31). Most likely, this refers to his second Roman imprisonment, which is attested by early traditions that supply details about the end of Paul's life. See introduction: Date.

1:9 a holy calling: Salvation is a process initiated by God, so that the grace we receive is entirely free and unmerited by our efforts (Rom 6:23; Tit 3:5). At the same time, God calls us to cooperate with his grace in order to become holy and reach our heavenly home (Phil 2:12; Heb 12:14) (CCC 1996, 2008). **ages ago:** The plan of salvation, now manifest through the historical events of Christ's life, was formulated in the hidden counsel of God before creation came into being (Jn 17:3–5; Eph 1:4).

1:12 whom I have believed: Christ, whom Paul calls his "Savior" (1:10). **that Day:** An abbreviated reference to the Day of Judgment (1:18; 4:8). **entrusted to me:** Paul did not invent the gospel, nor did he receive it from the original band of apostles. It was given to him directly from the risen Jesus (Gal 1:11–12).

ᵃ Or *what I have entrusted to him.*

47

have heard from me, in the faith and love which are in Christ Jesus; [14]guard the truth that has been entrusted to you by the Holy Spirit who dwells within us.

15 You are aware that all who are in Asia turned away from me, and among them Phy'gelus and Hermog'enes. [16]May the Lord grant mercy to the household of Onesiph'orus, for he often refreshed me; he was not ashamed of my chains, [17]but when he arrived in Rome he searched for me eagerly and found me—[18]may the Lord grant him to find mercy from the Lord on that Day—and you well know all the service he rendered at Ephesus.

A Good Soldier of Christ

2 You then, my son, be strong in the grace that is in Christ Jesus, [2]and what you have heard from me before many witnesses entrust to faithful men who will be able to teach others also. [3]Take your share of suffering as a good soldier of Christ Jesus. [4]No soldier on service gets entangled in civilian pursuits, since his aim is to satisfy the one who enlisted him. [5]An athlete is not crowned unless he competes according to the rules. [6]It is the hardworking farmer who ought to have the first share of the crops. [7]Think over what I say, for the Lord will grant you understanding in everything.

8 Remember Jesus Christ, risen from the dead, descended from David, as preached in my gospel, [9]the gospel for which I am suffering and wearing chains like a criminal. But the word of God is not chained. [10]Therefore I endure everything for the sake of the elect, that they also may obtain the salvation which in Christ Jesus goes with eternal glory. [11]The saying is sure:

If we have died with him, we shall also live with
    him;
[12]if we endure, we shall also reign with him;
    if we deny him, he also will deny us;
[13]if we are faithless, he remains faithful—
    for he cannot deny himself.

A Workman Approved by God

14 Remind them of this, and charge them before the Lord [b] to avoid disputing about words, which does no good, but only ruins the hearers.

1:14 guard the truth: The gospel that Paul received from Jesus is a sacred deposit now entrusted to Timothy for safekeeping (1 Tim 6:20). His highest responsibility is to preserve it from corruption, to defend it from attack, and to pass it along complete and intact to his successors (2:2) (CCC 84, 256). See introduction: *Themes and Characteristics*.

1:15 Asia: A Roman province in what is today southwestern Turkey. Its leading city, Ephesus, is the city where Timothy is presently stationed as bishop (1 Tim 1:3). Nothing specific is known of the cowardly Asian Christians who abandoned Paul for fear of persecution. **Phygelus and Hermogenes:** Otherwise unknown, but presumably known to Timothy.

1:16 Onesiphorus: He and his family may have lived in Ephesus (1:18). His diligent search for the imprisoned Paul was an expression of loyalty and courage, especially since Christians in Rome were at this time targets of fierce persecution (1:17). Some commentators infer that Onesiphorus died before 2 Timothy was written, since **(1)** Paul does not indicate that Onesiphorus is with him any longer; **(2)** he prays that the Lord will grant him mercy at the final Judgment (1:18); and **(3)** he asks Timothy to greet the household of Onesiphorus, but not Onesiphorus himself (4:19). If, in fact, Onesiphorus had died before Paul wrote this letter, then the apostle's prayer in 1:18 would be an early example of the Christian practice of praying for the dead.

2:1 my son: Paul is Timothy's spiritual father in the faith. See note on 1 Cor 4:15.

2:2 entrust to faithful men: Timothy is the second link in a chain of succession that stretches from the apostles of the first century to the bishops of the present day. Having received Paul's authority and mission, he is charged with passing on both the priestly ministry and the apostolic faith to the next generation. Timothy must transmit these traditions in the same way he received them from Paul: through public instruction, the sacramental imposition of hands, and the witness of his life (1:6, 13–14; 3:10; 1 Tim 5:22; 6:20). ● Apostolic succession takes place through the Sacrament of Holy Orders, when bishops receive and then transmit to others the fullness of their apostolic ministry. In this way, the authority that Jesus gave his apostles to preach, teach, administer the Sacraments, and govern the Church is passed on to successive generations until his glorious return (CCC 861–62, 1576).

2:3 share of suffering: Timothy must be brave and steadfast under trial, especially since the gospel he preaches will inevitably spark opposition from those offended by the Cross and uncomfortable with the harsh reality of sin (3:12; Gal 6:12). The commitment expected of him is exemplified in the soldier (2:4), the athlete (2:5), and the farmer (2:6), all of whom receive rewards for their toil and dedication.

2:8 Remember Jesus: Christ is the center of Paul's gospel. Through his natural birth in the line of King David and his miraculous rebirth in the Resurrection, the Jesus that Paul preaches is none other than the Messiah (CCC 436–37). ● In Paul's mind, Jesus fulfills God's covenant oath to raise up the Messiah from David's descendants and enthrone him over an eternal kingdom (2 Sam 7:12–16; Ps 89:3–4; 110:1; Lk 1:32–33). See note on Rom 1:3–4.

2:9 the word . . . not chained: Paul himself is shackled in prison, but his saving message continues to spread through trustworthy preachers such as Timothy. In this context, the "word of God" is equivalent to the gospel proclaimed by word of mouth (1 Thess 2:13; 1 Pet 1:25).

2:10 eternal glory: Everlasting life in heaven, where the saints enter the fullness of their inheritance (Mt 25:34; Col 3:23–24).

2:11–13 Possibly an excerpt from an ancient Christian hymn (CCC 2641). It sets forth in conditional propositions the blessings and curses that await us at the Judgment: those who persevere in faith will live and reign with Christ, but those who deny him will be disowned and disgraced in the end. Our ultimate certainty is that Christ will follow through on his promises and threats and so exercise his justice and mercy in perfect faithfulness to the terms of the New Covenant. Several of these statements echo Jesus' teaching in the Gospels (Mt 25:31–46; Mk 8:38; 13:13).

2:11 If we have died: Refers **(1)** to Baptism, where we die to sin and are filled with new life (Rom 6:2–4; CCC 1262–64), **(2)** to the Christian life, where we struggle with God's help to put to death our selfish and sinful inclinations (Rom 8:13), and **(3)** to death itself, which admits us into the presence of Christ our Judge (Phil 1:21) (CCC 1010).

2:14 avoid disputing: Timothy must silence errant teachers who are fascinated with useless speculation and become contentious when it comes to defending their private opinions before others (2:23; 1 Tim 1:3–7; 6:3–5). This is a matter of urgency since their novelties are already spreading like an infectious disease (2:17).

---

[b] Other ancient authorities read *God*.

[15]Do your best to present yourself to God as one approved, a workman who has no need to be ashamed, rightly handling the word of truth. [16]Avoid such godless chatter, for it will lead people into more and more ungodliness, [17]and their talk will eat its way like gangrene. Among them are Hymenae′us and Phile′tus, [18]who have swerved from the truth by holding that the resurrection is past already. They are upsetting the faith of some. [19]But God's firm foundation stands, bearing this seal: "The Lord knows those who are his," and, "Let every one who names the name of the Lord depart from iniquity."

20 In a great house there are not only vessels of gold and silver but also of wood and earthenware, and some for noble use, some for ignoble. [21]If any one purifies himself from what is ignoble, then he will be a vessel for noble use, consecrated and useful to the master of the house, ready for any good work. [22]So shun youthful passions and aim at righteousness, faith, love, and peace, along with those who call upon the Lord from a pure heart. [23]Have nothing to do with stupid, senseless controversies; you know that they breed quarrels. [24]And the Lord's servant must not be quarrelsome but kindly to every one, an apt teacher, forbearing, [25]correcting his opponents with gentleness. God may perhaps grant that they will repent and come to know the truth, [26]and they may escape from the snare of the devil, after being captured by him to do his will. [e]

Godlessness in the Last Days

3 But understand this, that in the last days there will come times of stress. [2]For men will be lovers of self, lovers of money, proud, arrogant, abusive, disobedient to their parents, ungrateful, unholy, [3]inhuman, implacable, slanderers, profligates, fierce, haters of good, [4]treacherous, reckless, swollen with conceit, lovers of pleasure rather than lovers of God, [5]holding the form of religion but denying the power of it. Avoid such people. [6]For among them are those who make their way into households and capture weak women, burdened with sins and swayed by various impulses, [7]who will listen to anybody and can never arrive at a knowledge of the truth. [8]As Jan′nes and Jam′bres opposed Moses, so these men also oppose the truth, men of corrupt mind and counterfeit faith; [9]but they will not get very far, for their folly will be plain to all, as was that of those two men.

Paul's Charge to Timothy

10 Now you have observed my teaching, my conduct, my aim in life, my faith, my patience, my love, my steadfastness, [11]my persecutions, my sufferings, what befell me at Antioch, at Ico′nium, and

---

2:19: Num 16:5; Is 26:13.   **3:8:** Ex 7:11.   **3:11:** Acts 13:14–52; 14:1–20; 16:1–5.

2:15 the word of truth: The gospel message, which is "heard" through preaching (Eph 1:13; Col 1:5). Uppermost in Paul's mind is the word of God orally proclaimed (1 Thess 2:13), not the word of God written in the Scriptures (Rom 15:4), though the latter is often central to Christian teaching and evangelism (3:16).

2:17 Hymenaeus: Possibly the same person Paul had already excommunicated for blasphemy (1 Tim 1:20). His partner **Philetus** is otherwise unknown.

2:18 the resurrection is past: The precise nature of this error is unclear. Perhaps false teachers affirmed a "spiritual resurrection" in connection with Baptism (Rom 6:3–4; CCC 1002) but denied the Pauline doctrine of a "bodily resurrection" of the whole person in the future (Rom 8:11; Phil 3:20–21; CCC 989). According to some, this denial smacks of early Gnosticism, an ancient heresy that reached its full development in the second and third centuries and was known to repudiate the body and the material world in general.

2:19 God's firm foundation: The gospel message, or perhaps the Church, which upholds the truth (1 Tim 3:15). **this seal:** Of the two quotations that follow, the first is from the Greek version of Num 16:5, and the second is drawn from an unknown source, though its wording resembles parts of Sir 35:3 and Is 26:13. • The context of the first excerpt is Korah's rebellion against Moses and the Aaronic priesthood, for which he and his fellow dissenters are destroyed by the Lord. Paul hints that a similar crisis is afoot in Ephesus, where Timothy is the legitimate priest and shepherd of God's people, while the false teachers are doomed to face God's judgment. **names the name of the Lord:** An act of prayer and worship (Gen 4:26; Acts 9:14; 1 Cor 1:2), unless the divine name is taken in vain (Ex 20:7; Lev 24:10–16).

2:22 shun youthful passions: Timothy is still a young man by ancient standards, probably in his mid-to-late thirties (1 Tim 4:12). Despite his age, he must flee from immaturity and pursue the virtues that befit a seasoned minister of the gospel.

2:24 forbearing: Timothy must deliver the truth at all times and refute errors whenever they arise. There is hope that straying sheep will return to the fold, so long as his pastoral teaching is matched by a life of integrity and patience (2:25; Jas 5:19–20).

3:1–9 Paul cautions Timothy about the moral depravity that is rampant among false teachers. Although they operate behind the mask of religion (3:5), they themselves are captives of bitterness, greed, pride, and a host of vile practices that offend God. Special concern is expressed for certain women who have already been victimized by their deceptions (3:6–7). Despite apparent success, Paul insists that their mischief will be exposed for what it truly is (3:9) (CCC 1852).

3:1 the last days: The final age of covenant history that began with the first coming of Jesus and will close with his Second Coming in glory (Acts 2:17; 1 Cor 10:11). Although the iniquity prevalent in these days will intensify as the end nears, it is already thriving here in the apostolic era (1 Tim 6:3–5).

3:8 Jannes and Jambres: Egyptian magicians who opposed Moses and Aaron (Ex 7:11). They are not named in the OT but are identified as such in Jewish tradition (e.g., in the Dead Sea Scrolls, CD 5, 18–19, and in an apocryphal work titled *Jannes and Jambres*).

3:10–14 Paul contrasts his own ministry of suffering with the self-indulgence of the false teachers (3:1–9). Timothy is to model himself on the example set by Paul, both in word and deed, so that past memories of the apostle will help him through the struggles that lie ahead (1:13; 2:8–10). Once a disciple of Paul, Timothy must now carry the torch as his successor.

3:11 Antioch . . . Iconium . . . Lystra: Cities in southern Asia Minor (modern Turkey) that Paul visited on his first missionary

---

[e] Or *by him, to do his* (that is, God's) *will.*

at Lystra, what persecutions I endured; yet from them all the Lord rescued me. [12]Indeed all who desire to live a godly life in Christ Jesus will be persecuted, [13]while evil men and impostors will go on from bad to worse, deceivers and deceived. [14]But as for you, continue in what you have learned and have firmly believed, knowing from whom you learned it [15]and how from childhood you have been acquainted with the Sacred Writings which are able to instruct you for salvation through faith in Christ Jesus. [16]All Scripture is inspired by God and[d] profitable for teaching, for reproof, for correction, and for training in righteousness, [17]that the man of God may be complete, equipped for every good work.

4 I charge you in the presence of God and of Christ Jesus who is to judge the living and the dead, and by his appearing and his kingdom: [2]preach the word, be urgent in season and out of season, convince, rebuke, and exhort, be unfailing in patience and in teaching. [3]For the time is coming when people will not endure sound teaching, but having itching ears they will accumulate for themselves teachers to suit their own likings, [4]and will turn away from listening to the truth and wander into myths. [5]As for you, always be steady, endure suffering, do the work of an evangelist, fulfil your ministry.

6 For I am already on the point of being sacrificed; the time of my departure has come. [7]I have fought the good fight, I have finished the race, I have kept the faith. [8]From now on there is laid up for me the crown of righteousness, which the Lord, the righteous judge, will award to me on that Day,

---

journey (Acts 13:14–14:23). Timothy, as a resident of Lystra, probably embraced the Christian faith at this time and may have witnessed the persecutions that Paul endured there (Acts 14:19; 16:1).

3:12 will be persecuted: Antagonism toward the gospel often strikes those who preach it. The inevitability of Christian suffering is a recurring theme in this letter (1:8; 2:3; 4:5) and in the NT generally (Jn 16:2–3; Acts 14:22; 1 Pet 4:12–14). ● Persecution is not only what attacks Christian piety by sword, fire, and torments. Persecution is also inflicted through personal conflict, the perversity of the disobedient, and the sharp point of slanderous tongues (St. Leo the Great, *Letters* 167).

3:15 the Sacred Writings: I.e., the writings of the OT. The NT had not yet been written when Timothy was a young boy. Jewish children often began instruction in the Torah at age five (Mishnah, *Aboth* 5, 21). **for salvation:** The books of the OT point the way to Christ (Rom 1:2–3) and continue to instruct his disciples for life in the New Covenant (Rom 15:4) (CCC 121–23, 128–30).

---

[d] Or *Every Scripture inspired by God is also.*

Word Study

Inspired by God (2 Tim 3:16)

Theopneustos (Gk.): A compound adjective that means "God-breathed" and is found only here in the NT. It is formed from the noun "God" (*Theos*) and a verb meaning "blow" or "breathe out" (*pneō*). Applied to the Scriptures, it means that everything written down in the Bible has been breathed forth from the mouth of the Lord. God is thus the ultimate source of Scripture and, indeed, its principal Author. The similar passage in 2 Pet 1:20–21 adds to this teaching that God collaborated with human authors in producing the biblical books. Inspiration thus means that the Holy Spirit acted in and through the human writers as they wrote, so that the words they left behind are truly sacred expressions of God's instructions to his People. Finally, because the Bible enshrines the very words of God, its message is as truthful as God himself is (Jn 17:17; Tit 1:1–2) and is thus a reliable guide for Christian living, able to instruct us for every good work (2 Tim 3:17) (CCC 105–8).

3:16 All Scripture is inspired: Some prefer to translate this "All inspired Scripture", which is grammatically possible but contextually and statistically unlikely. For one thing, it would allow the possibility that some Scriptures might not be inspired, and neither Paul nor any other theologian in the early Church accepted such a proposition. Also, parallel constructions in Greek almost always treat the second modifier as a predicate (Scripture is inspired) rather than an attributive (inspired Scripture).

3:17 complete: Paul extols Scripture as a preeminent guide for the moral life. He does not claim, however, that Scripture supplies us with comprehensive instruction in all matters of Christian doctrine, worship, and ecclesial government. Besides the divine authority of the biblical books, he also acknowledges the authority of apostolic tradition (1 Cor 11:1; 2 Thess 2:15) and sees the Church, built on the foundation of Christ and the apostles (1 Cor 3:11; Eph 2:20), as the bearer of God's truth to the world (1 Tim 3:15). For the role of tradition and the teaching office of the Magisterium, see notes on Jn 14:26, 16:13, and 2 Thess 2:15. ● Sacred Scripture is extremely profitable for the soul. Like a tree planted near a stream, the soul that is watered by Scripture grows hearty and bears fruit in due season. It is fitted with leaves that are always green, with actions pleasing to God (St. John of Damascus, *Orthodox Faith* 4, 17).

4:1 in the presence of God: Paul speaks as if testifying in a courtroom where God is present and Jesus Christ presides as judge. He issues a final and solemn appeal for Timothy to fulfill his mission as a teacher of God's people.

4:2 in season and out of season: Timothy must proclaim the gospel, making the most of his time to correct or encourage his flock as each situation demands (Eph 5:16).

4:4 wander into myths: Already a problem in Ephesus (1 Tim 1:4; 4:7), where erring teachers have exchanged the revealed truth of God for the uncertainties of their own speculation—and hear only what suits their liking (4:3).

4:6 the point of being sacrificed: Or "being poured out as a libation". The description alludes to the cultic liturgy of Israel, where daily drink offerings of wine were poured out at the base of the Temple altar (Ex 29:38–40; Num 28:7). Evoking this imagery, Paul sees martyrdom as an act of sacrifice and liturgical worship (Phil 2:17) (CCC 2473). **my departure:** A metaphor for death, which in Paul's case is both imminent and personally desirable (Phil 1:23). According to tradition, Paul was condemned during the Neronian persecution that began in the mid 60s and was beheaded just outside the city of Rome along the Ostian Way.

4:8 crown of righteousness: The reward of everlasting righteousness (Gal 5:5) that awaits the saints, who have persevered in the grace of God (Jas 1:12; 1 Pet 5:4). The image alludes to the garland or victory wreath used to crown winning

and not only to me but also to all who have loved his appearing.

Personal Instructions

9 Do your best to come to me soon. [10]For Demas, in love with this present world, has deserted me and gone to Thessaloni'ca; Crescens has gone to Galatia,• Titus to Dalmatia. [11]Luke alone is with me. Get Mark and bring him with you; for he is very useful in serving me. [12]Tych'icus I have sent to Ephesus. [13]When you come, bring the cloak that I left with Carpus at Tro'as, also the books, and above all the parchments. [14]Alexander the coppersmith did me great harm; the Lord will pay him back for his deeds. [15]Beware of him yourself, for he strongly opposed our message. [16]At my first defense no one took my part; all deserted me. May it not be charged against them! [17]But the Lord stood by me and gave me strength to proclaim the word fully, that all the Gentiles might hear it. So I was rescued from the lion's mouth. [18]The Lord will rescue me from every evil and save me for his heavenly kingdom. To him be the glory for ever and ever. Amen.

Final Greetings and Benediction

19 Greet Prisca and Aqui'la, and the household of Onesiph'orus. [20]Eras'tus remained at Corinth; Troph'imus I left ill at Mile'tus. [21]Do your best to come before winter. Eubu'lus sends greetings to you, as do Pudens and Linus and Claudia and all the brethren.

22 The Lord be with your spirit. Grace be with you.

---

athletes in the ancient Olympics (1 Cor 9:25). Paul's confidence that such a reward awaits him rests on his sense of accomplishment, since after 30 years of ministry, toil, and suffering, he has remained firm in the faith without straying from the course set for him by Christ (4:7; Acts 20:24). He was not nearly so assured of his salvation while the race was still in progress (1 Cor 9:16). • Is not a crown the reward of good deeds? Yet, this is possible only because God accomplishes good works in men. It is through his mercy that we perform the goods works to which the crown is awarded (St. Augustine, *On Grace and Free Will* 21). **that Day:** The Day of Judgment. **his appearing:** Either the future return of Christ in glory (4:1) or, possibly, his first coming in the flesh (1:10).

4:9 come to me soon: The nearness of Paul's death adds a sense of urgency to his request (1:4). Timothy must not delay because the onset of winter (4:21) will make sea travel impossible, and Paul needs his cloak to stay warm in prison (4:13).

4:10 Demas: One of Paul's associates, but one whose attachment to worldly comforts tore him away from the apostle. He was once a loyal companion (Col 4:14; Philem 24).

4:11 Luke: The physician and evangelist who wrote the Gospel of Luke and its sequel, the Book of Acts. He traveled with Paul on parts of his second and third missionary tours and was present with him at his first Roman imprisonment (Col 4:14; Philem 24). See introduction to Acts: *Author*. **Mark:** John Mark, the evangelist who wrote the Gospel of Mark. Once estranged from Paul for abandoning his missionary team (Acts 13:13; 15:39), he later rejoined the apostle's company and was present with him at his first Roman imprisonment (Col 4:10; Philem 24).

4:12 Tychicus: One of Paul's personal couriers (Eph 6:21; Col 4:7-9; Tit 3:12).

4:13 books . . . parchments: Two forms of writing material, the first referring to papyrus scrolls and the second to sheets made from animal skins. No hint is given of their contents, but they may have included Paul's personal copies of OT books.

4:14 Alexander the coppersmith: Possibly a heretic Paul excommunicated for blasphemy (1 Tim 1:20).

4:17 strength to proclaim: Paul's preliminary hearing before the Roman court was disappointing because his companions abandoned him; nevertheless, it was successful because an opportunity was given to expound the gospel in the imperial capital (CCC 2471-72). **the lion's mouth:** Metaphorically, "a verdict of condemnation". Because Paul was a Roman citizen, he would not have been thrown to the lions in the Roman circus.

4:19 Prisca and Aquila: A distinguished Christian couple who worked alongside Paul (Acts 18:2-3) and went on to minister in the churches of Rome (Rom 16:3-5) and Ephesus (Acts 18:24-26; 1 Cor 16:19). The name "Prisca" is also spelled "Priscilla".

4:21 Linus: Quite possibly Peter's first successor as pope. Saint Irenaeus gives us a running list of the bishops of Rome from the apostolic age down to the late second century, and the first in succession after Peter is named "Linus" (*Against Heresies* 3, 3, 3).

4:22 Grace be with you: All the Pastoral Epistles end with a benediction that has the word "you" in the plural (1 Tim 6:21; Tit 3:15). This suggests that while Paul addressed his letters to Timothy and Titus privately, he intended his correspondence to be read publicly to the congregations under their care.

• Other ancient authorities read *Gaul.*

STUDY QUESTIONS
2 Timothy

Chapter 1

For understanding
1. **1:5.** Who are the members of Timothy's family named here? What do we know about them? Why does Paul mention them?
2. **1:7.** What is Timothy urged to do? What is the purpose of Paul's exhortation?
3. **1:8.** To which imprisonment of Paul does this verse refer? How do we know, since it is not otherwise recorded in the NT?
4. **1:9.** Since salvation is a process initiated by God, what does Paul say about the grace we receive for it? What does God call us to do? How long has the plan of salvation been in God's mind?

For application
1. **1:5.** Have any members of your family had a positive influence on your faith? If you are a parent or a teacher, how do you want to influence the faith of those for whom you are responsible?
2. **1:7.** How does timidity differ from natural shyness? Has timidity (not shyness) ever affected your spiritual life? What three virtues does Paul say the Holy Spirit has given you? How do you think the Holy Spirit wants you to apply them in your circumstances?
3. **1:8-12.** If you were accused of being a Christian, would there be enough evidence to convict you? Has fear or shame ever inhibited you from witnessing to your faith? What have you done to conquer that fear or shame?
4. **1:13-14.** Whether you participate directly in the work of the Magisterium or not, what is your role in guarding the truth of the faith? Have you ever seen the truth contradicted? What might you do to defend it?

Chapter 2

For understanding
1. **2:2.** Where does Timothy fit in the chain of apostolic succession? What charges has he received in this regard? How does apostolic succession take place?
2. **2:11-13.** What is the possible source of these verses? What propositions are set forth here? What is our ultimate certainty?
3. **2:18.** How might false teachers have misconstrued the doctrine of the resurrection? What did they deny about it? How might their teachings have been a distortion of Paul's own? What ancient heresy does this resemble?
4. **2:19.** What are the sources of the two quotations that Paul sees on the Church's foundation? What is the point of the citation from Numbers 16 for the Ephesian Church?

For application
1. **2:3-7.** How would you describe a "radical Christian"? Do these verses match your description? What kind of "understanding" (v. 7) do you think you still need about these things?
2. **2:8-13.** Have you ever come close to denying Christ? What got you through the experience? Can you look back on the experience and say that Christ has ever denied you?
3. **2:20-22.** Regardless of your age, what sorts of "youthful passions" have you had to contend with? As you learn to "shun" these passions and acquire the virtues listed here, what changes do you notice in the opportunities the Lord gives you to serve him?
4. **2:24-26.** What do these verses suggest about how you might approach friends or family members who have strayed from the Christian way of life? Paul mentions correcting opponents with gentleness; what is your approach to correcting others? What was the most effective and fruitful correction you have ever received, and what does it tell you about your own approach?

Chapter 3

For understanding

1. **3:8.** Who are Jannes and Jambres? Are they identified by name in the OT?
2. **3:15.** To what does the expression "the Sacred Writings" refer? When did Jewish children normally start studying the Torah? What does Paul maintain about the books of the OT?
3. **Word Study: Inspired by God (3:16).** What does the Greek word for "inspired" mean? From what root words does it come? What does the word mean when applied to Scripture? What understanding does the passage from 2 Peter add to this? Finally, what does the fact that the Bible enshrines the very words of God mean for those of us who read it?

For application

1. **3:1-5.** How do Paul's characterizations apply to the environment in which you live? If his description fits, what is your response to it?
2. **3:10-14.** Who are your role models in the Christian life? What has their behavior taught you about how you should behave? How can you be a role model for others younger than yourself?
3. **3:15.** How well acquainted are you with Sacred Scripture? What is your greatest fear when it comes to understanding Scripture? How have you tried to remove that fear?
4. **3:16-17.** What difference has the reading of Scripture made on your life? Paul mentions several things for which Scripture is useful. Have these helped you personally to be "equipped for every good work"?

Chapter 4

For understanding

1. **4:6.** To what does the expression "the point of being sacrificed" allude? Why does Paul evoke this imagery? What does "my departure" mean? According to tradition, how did Paul "depart"?
2. **4:8.** To what does a "crown of righteousness" allude? Of what is it symbolic? On what does Paul's confidence rest? When was he not nearly so assured?
3. **4:11.** Who is Luke, and what relationship does he have with Paul? Who is Mark, and what is his relationship with Paul?
4. **4:17.** Why was Paul's preliminary hearing before the Roman court disappointing? Why does Paul refer to "the lion's mouth" in this verse?

For application

1. **4:1-2.** Why do you think Paul is so insistent about the urgency of preaching the word "in season and out of season"? Would he feel that same urgency today? Assuming that you "preach by example", how do you preach (or evangelize, or share) using words? If you do not do that, what prevents you?
2. **4:3-4.** How can a person keep an open mind and yet reject unsound teaching? Why is a person who rejects unsound teaching not being "narrow-minded" in the usual sense of that term?
3. **4:5.** Paul urges Timothy to do his job as a bishop. How does his admonition apply to you? Given your state in life, how do you maintain steadiness, endure suffering, evangelize, and fulfill your ministry?

INTRODUCTION TO THE
LETTER OF SAINT PAUL TO TITUS

Author Titus claims to be a letter from the Apostle Paul (1:1), as do the other Pastoral Epistles (1 Tim 1:1; 2 Tim 1:1). Christian writers accepted this claim from earliest times, and it was not until the nineteenth century that biblical scholars began to dispute and then deny the Pauline authorship of Titus. Many exegetes today continue to attribute this epistle to a devoted follower of Paul who wrote a decade or more after the apostle's death. Nevertheless, reasons for upholding its authenticity remain strong, and there is much in the letter that lends credence to the tradition that Paul himself composed the epistle. Indeed, Titus gives us valuable insights into Paul's ministry and movements during the final years of his life that we would not otherwise know. See introduction to 1 Timothy: *Author*.

Date It is difficult to establish an exact date for Titus. Information within the letter about Paul's situation is spare, and the little there is does not fit into the travel itinerary of his three missionary journeys described in the Book of Acts. This has led many to posit that Paul must have embarked on a fourth missionary tour in the eastern Mediterranean sometime *after* his Roman imprisonment recorded in Acts 28:16 (from A.D. 60 to 62) yet *before* his martyrdom a few years later (ca. A.D. 67). The possibility of a fourth missionary campaign in the mid 60s is accepted by many scholars and is supported by the testimony of early Christian tradition. This would mean that Paul wrote Titus sometime between A.D. 63 and 66, around the same time he wrote 1 Timothy. Scholars who deny the Pauline authorship of the letter tend to date it much later, between A.D. 80 and 110.

Destination and Purpose The letter was sent to Titus on the Mediterranean island of Crete. Although Crete had an established Jewish community (1:10; Acts 2:11), its inhabitants were mostly Gentiles and pagans infamous for their moral decadence (1:12). Paul and Titus had previously evangelized parts of the island together, but Titus was left behind while Paul continued to travel. Titus was charged with organizing the converts into communities and ensuring that elders or presbyters (i.e., priests) were appointed to lead the flock (1:5). Paul now writes to encourage Titus and to authorize his spiritual and organizational efforts (2:15). He places full confidence in Titus, who has already proven himself a capable delegate in even the most sensitive situations in Corinth (2 Cor 7:6, 13–15; 8:16–23). Once Titus fulfills his mission and is re-

lieved of his duty by a replacement, he is to rejoin Paul in Nicopolis for the winter (3:12).

Themes and Characteristics The letter to Titus shares much in common with 1 Timothy, although its instructions are less detailed and its tone is less personal. Still, both letters are addressed to young bishops on temporary assignment: Titus on the island of Crete (1:5) and Timothy in the city of Ephesus (1 Tim 1:3). Both of these men have been handed the challenging task of supervising communities that are threatened by false teaching (1:10–16; 1 Tim 1:3–7), in need of sound doctrine (2:1; 1 Tim 4:11–16), and lacking in qualified leadership (1:5–9; 1 Tim 3:1–13). These are men Paul can trust. These are the men he is grooming to continue his ministry after his death.

The themes of the letter follow the instructions that Paul is giving to Titus, whose mission is to organize both the pastoral leadership and the personal lives of the believers on Crete. **(1)** *Pastoral Leadership*. The first assignment given to Titus is to ordain qualified elders (priests) in every town, lest Christians on the island be like wandering sheep without shepherds to lead them (1:5). This is not to be done arbitrarily but with discernment. In Paul's mind, the only fitting candidates for spiritual leadership are men of proven character and deep convictions (1:7–8). A practical element is also involved in this, and so Titus must take account of how well a prospective clergyman manages his own family and household when considering his selection (1:6). As a final note, Paul stresses that candidates must be competent instructors and defenders of the truth, able to lead the faithful as teachers and apologists (1:9). This is all the more necessary in Crete, where dangerous teachings are already taking hold in the Christian communities spread across the island (1:10–16). **(2)** *Personal Living*. Paul reasons that because Christianity is advertised to the world through our actions, it is important that our behavior be consistent with our beliefs, lest the Church of God be discredited in the eyes of nonbelievers. There is thus a strong emphasis in Titus that believers should be zealous for every good work (2:7, 14; 3:1, 8, 14). This includes not only acts of charity toward fellow Christians (2:2–10), but also a respectful posture toward government authorities and fellow Cretans more generally (3:1–2). The immediate aim of such works is to assist the needy (3:14), while their ultimate purpose is to honor the Lord Jesus in anticipation of his glorious return (2:11–13).

OUTLINE OF THE LETTER OF SAINT PAUL TO TITUS

1. **Opening Address (1:1–4)**

2. **Christian Leadership (1:5–16)**
   A. Appointing Shepherds in Crete (1:5)
   B. Qualifications for Pastors (1:6–9)
   C. The Problem of False Teachers (1:10–16)

3. **Christian Living (2:1–3:11)**
   A. Instructions for All Ages (2:1–10)
   B. Foundation of the Christian Commitment (2:11–15)
   C. Life with and without Christ (3:1–7)
   D. Avoiding Trouble and Troublemakers (3:8–11)

4. **Conclusion (3:12–15)**
   A. Final Instructions (3:12–14)
   B. Benediction (3:15)

THE LETTER OF SAINT PAUL TO

TITUS

Salutation

1 Paul, a servant[a] of God and an apostle of Jesus Christ, to further the faith of God's elect and their knowledge of the truth which accords with godliness, [2]in hope of eternal life which God, who never lies, promised ages ago [3]and at the proper time manifested in his word through the preaching with which I have been entrusted by command of God our Savior;

4 To Titus, my true child in a common faith:
Grace and peace from God the Father and Christ Jesus our Savior.

Titus in Crete

5 This is why I left you in Crete, that you might amend what was defective, and appoint elders in every town as I directed you, [6]if any man is blameless, the husband of one wife, and his children are believers and not open to the charge of debauchery and not being insubordinate. [7]For a bishop, as God's steward, must be blameless; he must not be arrogant or quick-tempered or a drunkard or violent or greedy for gain, [8]but hospitable, a lover of goodness, master of himself, upright, holy, and self-controlled; [9]he must hold firm to the sure word as taught, so that he may be able to give instruction in sound doctrine and also to confute those who contradict it. [10]For there are many insubordinate men, empty talkers and deceivers, especially the circumcision party; [11]they must be silenced, since they are upsetting whole families by teaching for base gain what they have no right to teach. [12]One of themselves, a prophet of their own, said, "Cretans are always liars, evil beasts, lazy gluttons." [13]This testimony is true. Therefore rebuke them sharply, that

---

1:1 Paul: The author (and sender) is always named first, according to the ancient letter format. As a servant, Paul devotes all of himself and his energies to the service of the Lord, and, as an apostle (Rom 1:1), he is commissioned to preach that God is reconciling the world to himself through Jesus Christ (2 Cor 5:18–20).

1:2 God . . . never lies: Hope that is anchored in God will never be disappointed, for his word is ever truthful, and his promises are entirely trustworthy (Num 23:19; Jn 17:17; Heb 6:17–18). The same cannot be said for the pagan Cretans (1:12) or for the devil, the father of every falsehood (Jn 8:44) (CCC 214–17). ● Let us bind ourselves to him who is ever true and just in his judgments. He who has forbidden us to lie can much less be a liar himself, for deception is impossible for God (St. Clement of Rome, *1 Clement* 27).

1:3 our Savior: A title three times given to God the Father (1:3; 2:10; 3:4) and three times applied to Christ the Son (1:4; 2:13; 3:6). See note on 1 Tim 1:1.

1:4 Titus: A Gentile believer (Gal 2:3) and a devoted member of Paul's missionary team (2 Cor 8:23). He is never mentioned by name in the Book of Acts. According to the Pastoral Epistles, Titus was in Dalmatia near the end of Paul's life (2 Tim 4:10), and, according to tradition, he eventually returned to Crete to minister to the churches on the island until his death. **my true child:** The spiritual sonship of Titus points to the spiritual fatherhood of Paul. It may mean that Paul converted Titus to the Christian faith, as he had the Corinthians (1 Cor 4:14–15), or that Paul ordained Titus to the pastoral ministry, as he had done with Timothy (1 Tim 4:14; 2 Tim 1:6). In Scripture, spiritual fatherhood is connected with the priestly ministry (Judg 17:10) as it passed from fathers to sons under the Old Covenant (Ex 40:12–15) (CCC 1541). See note on 1 Cor 4:15.

1:5 I left you in Crete: Implies that Paul and Titus evangelized the island together before the apostle's departure. Nothing more is known of this missionary effort. **appoint elders:** An essential step in organizing and stabilizing young Christian communities (Acts 14:23). That Titus is charged with this duty indicates that he is already a bishop and thus qualified to ordain others to priestly ministry by the sacramental imposition of hands (1 Tim 5:22) (CCC 1573, 1576). Notice that in this letter, as in the earliest days of the Church, the titles "elder" (1:5) and "bishop" (1:7) seem to be used interchangeably (Acts 20:17, 28). See notes on 1 Tim 3:1 and 1 Tim 4:14.

1:6 husband of one wife: I.e., married only once during his lifetime. Paul allows younger widows to remarry (1 Tim 5:14). However, he holds prospective clergymen to a more stringent standard (1 Tim 3:2, 12). On possible reasons for this, see note on 1 Tim 3:2.

1:7 God's steward: A steward is an administrator over the household of another. Paul is suggesting that if a candidate for pastoral ministry is unable to manage his own home and children, he is unfit to oversee the affairs of God's household, which is the Church (1 Tim 3:15). Titus is to look for men whose family life (1:6) and personal life (1:7–8) are well ordered and whose zeal for sound doctrine is beyond question (1:9). For a similar list of qualifications, see 1 Tim 3:1–7.

1:10 the circumcision party: Jewish Christian troublemakers in Crete. They adhered to unscriptural myths (1:14), made speculative conjectures about biblical genealogies, and haggled over minor points of the Mosaic Law (3:9). Because their teaching was unsettling the faith of young believers, Titus is authorized to silence (1:11) and rebuke them (1:13).

1:12 Cretans are . . . gluttons: A quotation from the Cretan poet Epimenides, who lived in the sixth century B.C. He was revered as a prophet by several writers in antiquity (not necessarily by Paul). Cretans were so noted for untruthfulness that the verb "to Cretanize" meant "to lie or cheat" in Greek literature. Paul apparently thinks their infamous reputation is justified, for he declares that the poet's proverb is still "true" in his own day (1:13). Paul cites another quotation from

---

[a] Or *slave*.

they may be sound in the faith, [14]instead of giving heed to Jewish myths or to commands of men who reject the truth. [15]To the pure all things are pure, but to the corrupt and unbelieving nothing is pure; their very minds and consciences are corrupted. [16]They profess to know God, but they deny him by their deeds; they are detestable, disobedient, unfit for any good deed.

Teach Sound Doctrine

2 But as for you, teach what befits sound doctrine. [2]Bid the older men be temperate, serious, sensible, sound in faith, in love, and in steadfastness. [3]Bid the older women likewise to be reverent in behavior, not to be slanderers or slaves to drink; they are to teach what is good, [4]and so train the young women to love their husbands and children, [5]to be sensible, chaste, domestic, kind, and submissive to their husbands, that the word of God may not be discredited. [6]Likewise urge the younger men to control themselves. [7]Show yourself in all respects a model of good deeds, and in your teaching show integrity, gravity, [8]and sound speech

that cannot be censured, so that an opponent may be put to shame, having nothing evil to say of us. [9]Bid slaves to be submissive to their masters and to give satisfaction in every respect; they are not to talk back, [10]nor to pilfer, but to show entire and true fidelity, so that in everything they may adorn the doctrine of God our Savior.

11 For the grace of God has appeared for the salvation of all men, [12]training us to renounce irreligion and worldly passions, and to live sober, upright, and godly lives in this world, [13]awaiting our blessed hope, the appearing of the glory of our great God and Savior [c] Jesus Christ, [14]who gave himself for us to redeem us from all iniquity and to purify for himself a people of his own who are zealous for good deeds.

15 Declare these things; exhort and reprove with all authority. Let no one disregard you.

Maintain Good Deeds

3 Remind them to be submissive to rulers and authorities, to be obedient, to be ready for any honest work, [2]to speak evil of no one, to avoid

---

2:14: Ps 130:8; Ezek 37:23; Deut 14:2.

Epimenides in Acts 17:28. ● One who is learned in Sacred Scripture accepts the truth wherever he finds it. This is why Paul, on several occasions, refers to the sayings of pagans. It does not follow that all their teaching is approved, but what is good is drawn out and retained. For truth comes from the Holy Spirit, no matter who speaks it (St. Thomas Aquinas, *Commentary on Titus* 1, 3).

1:14 Jewish myths: Probably legends about biblical heroes that are preserved in Jewish apocryphal writings near the end of the OT period (1 Tim 1:4; 4:7).

1:15 To the pure: Reads like a response to the "Jewish" propaganda in the preceding verse (1:14). If so, perhaps troublemakers were promoting the dietary distinctions between clean and unclean foods (Lev 11:1–47) as well as the non-biblical laws of purity formulated within Pharisaic Judaism (compare the "commands of men" in 1:14 with Mk 7:1–8). Paul insists, however, that because Christians are themselves purified (2:14), they are not bound to follow the purity legislation of the Old Covenant or Jewish tradition in general (Acts 10:15; Rom 14:14). Notice that Paul is addressing a misunderstanding about ritual purity and defilement; he is not saying that believers are immune to the pollution of sin.

2:1–10 Titus must counsel believers in accordance with their age (young/old), gender (men/women), and station in life (slave/free). Faith and life are meant to form a unity, and so the behavior Paul expects of them is part of "sound doctrine" (2:1). In effect, Paul wants the Cretan believers to rise above the dishonorable reputation that plagues their country (1:12), lest the gospel be discredited before unbelievers (2:5).

2:1 But as for you: The Greek is emphatic, drawing a sharp contrast between Titus, whose mission is to propagate true doctrine, and the Jewish teachers, whose destructive ideas were denounced in the preceding context (1:10–16).

2:7 model of good deeds: Titus' own life must be consistent with his preaching, otherwise opponents will make his personal defects a cause for public disgrace (2:8).

2:9 slaves: Slavery was an accepted institution in Roman society. Paul did not attack it directly in his letters, but he sought to improve the relationship between masters and slaves and stressed that both stand on an equal footing in Christ (Gal 3:28; Col 3:22—4:1). Here he implies that the dependability of

slaves will help to advertise the gospel to the world. See note on Eph 6:5.

2:11–14 This paragraph spells out the basis of Paul's ethical instructions in the previous ten verses. Emphasis is placed on the purpose of grace, not only to cleanse us of unrighteousness (2:14), but to raise us up to a higher standard of moral living (2:12).

2:11 the salvation of all: The grace of Christ invites every person and nation into the covenant family of God. See note on 1 Tim 2:4.

2:13 our blessed hope: The return of Jesus in glory, which Paul often describes as the "appearing" of Christ from heaven (2 Thess 2:8; 1 Tim 6:14; 2 Tim 4:1, 8; CCC 1130, 1404). **our great God and Savior Jesus:** The syntax of this statement in Greek indicates that Paul is asserting the divinity of Jesus (Jn 10:33–38; Col 2:9; 2 Pet 1:1). Less likely translations make a distinction between God and Christ in this verse (see textual note c).

2:14 to redeem us: I.e., to purchase us from the bondage of sin and to purify us for a life of divine sonship. See note on Eph 1:7. **people of his own:** The expression is taken from the Greek OT. ● Both Ex 19:5 and Deut 7:6 use these words to describe Israel as Yahweh's special possession by covenant. The nation was set apart as a holy and priestly people called to draw other nations closer to God (Deut 4:6–8; Is 49:6). But since the persistence of sin and weakness prevented Israel from fulfilling this vocation under the Old Covenant, Christ came to reconstitute his covenant people in the Church (1 Pet 2:9) and to empower them to fulfill the mission once given to Israel (Mt 5:14–16). Paul's words are also reminiscent of the New Covenant oracles of Ezekiel, especially Ezek 37:23.

2:15 exhort and reprove: This is the third time Paul challenges Titus to make an aggressive stand against the false teachers who plague the Cretan communities (1:11, 13).

3:1 submissive to rulers: Titus must remind his flock that public life is to be as shaped by the gospel as is private life. A Christian's allegiance to civil government is part of this, as is working for justice and the betterment of society. The saints, Paul is saying, must also be exemplary citizens (Rom 13:1–7; 1 Pet 2:13–17; CCC 2238–42).

3:2 be gentle: Or "meek". Paul asks believers to bear injuries and restrain anger even when provoked, so that Christian charity will shine out in even the most hostile environments.

---

[c] Or *of the great God and our Savior.*

quarreling, to be gentle, and to show perfect courtesy toward all men. [3]For we ourselves were once foolish, disobedient, led astray, slaves to various passions and pleasures, passing our days in malice and envy, hated by men and hating one another; [4]but when the goodness and loving kindness of God our Savior appeared, [5]he saved us, not because of deeds done by us in righteousness, but in virtue of his own mercy, by the washing of regeneration and renewal in the Holy Spirit, [6]which he poured out upon us richly through Jesus Christ our Savior, [7]so that we might be justified by his grace and become heirs in hope of eternal life. [8]The saying is sure.

I desire you to insist on these things, so that those who have believed in God may be careful to apply themselves to good deeds; [d] these are excellent and profitable to men. [9]But avoid stupid controversies, genealogies, dissensions, and quarrels over the law, for they are unprofitable and futile. [10]As for a man who is factious, after admonishing him once or twice, have nothing more to do with him, [11]knowing that such a person is perverted and sinful; he is self-condemned.

Final Messages and Benediction

12 When I send Ar'temas or Tych'icus to you, do your best to come to me at Nicop'olis, for I have decided to spend the winter there. [13]Do your best to speed Ze'nas the lawyer and Apol'los on their way; see that they lack nothing. [14]And let our people learn to apply themselves to good deeds, [d] so as to help cases of urgent need, and not to be unfruitful.

15 All who are with me send greetings to you. Greet those who love us in the faith.

Grace be with you all.

Jesus exemplified this virtue in his own life (Mt 11:29; 2 Cor 10:1).

3:3 once foolish: A snapshot of the moral and spiritual depravity that plagues the human race. More detailed reflections on this condition are found in Rom 1:18–32 and Eph 4:17–19.

3:5 he saved us: Salvation springs entirely from the mercy and grace of God. It is not an achievement on our part or a payment rendered for services. Apart from grace, even our most heroic efforts to please God fall short of his glory and his plan for our lives (Rom 6:23). Both the *faith* to believe in Christ and *grace* to live the gospel are undeserved gifts (Eph 2:8; Phil 1:29). Only after God has bestowed these gifts can we begin to please our heavenly Father through a lifetime of service and good works (2:14; Eph 2:10; Heb 11:6) (CCC 1996–2002).

---

[d] Or *enter honorable occupations.*

Word Study

Regeneration (Tit 3:5)

Palingenesia (Gk.): refers to a "rebirth", "restoration", or "renewal". The term is used only twice in the Bible, here and in Mt 19:28, though it appears several times in non-biblical writings. Stoic philosophers, for instance, believed that a renewed world order would emerge after a fiery purgation of the cosmos. The Jewish philosopher Philo of Alexandria spoke in a similar way about the rebirth of the world after the flood in Noah's day (*Life of Moses* 2, 65). The Jewish historian Josephus employs the term for the restoration of Israel after the tragedy of exile (*Antiquities* 11, 66). In Titus, Paul links the idea of regeneration with a baptismal washing that cleanses us of sin and gives us a new birth into the family of God (cf. Jn 3:5; Eph 5:26). He is saying that the washing of the body is an efficacious sign of the invisible work of the Spirit, whose action in the sacrament renews and renovates our souls with divine grace (Acts 2:38; 1 Pet 3:21) (CCC 1215, 1265).

3:7 justified: Cleansed from sin and made righteous in the sight of God. See word study: *Justified* at Rom 2:13. **become heirs:** Through the grace of divine adoption, which makes us children of God and thus heirs of all that the Father desires to give us (Rom 8:14–17; Gal 4:3–7). **hope of eternal life:** Even now we possess eternal life in the form of grace (Eph 2:5; 1 Jn 5:13), but the full possession of glory in heaven is a future hope rather than a present assurance (1:2; Rom 8:24–25; Eph 1:13–14, 18; 1 Tim 6:18–19). ● If someone asks whether we have been saved by Baptism, one should not deny it, for the apostle says as much. But if he should ask whether that same washing has already saved us in every respect, one should have to say no, for the apostle says we are saved "in hope" (St. Augustine, *Answer to Two Pelagian Letters* 3, 3).

3:9 genealogies . . . quarrels over the law: Disputes of this kind erupted among the Jewish controversialists about whom Titus was warned in 1:10–16.

3:10–11 A pastoral plan for dealing with divisive Christians. Attempts must first be made to correct the offender and warn him of the consequences of his actions. Should he persist in his stubborn ways, Titus is to exclude him from the community's life and liturgy (Mt 18:15–18). Concrete examples of this corrective discipline are found in 1 Cor 5:1–5 and 1 Tim 1:19–20 (CCC 1463).

3:10 a man who is factious: The Greek expression would later become a technical term for a "heretic" whose teachings were contrary to the truth and condemned by the Church.

3:12 Artemas or Tychicus: One of these two men was to be Titus' replacement, freeing him to rejoin Paul for the winter. The former is otherwise unknown in the NT, but the latter is mentioned several times in Paul's letters (Eph 6:21; Col 4:7; 2 Tim 4:12). **Nicopolis:** Probably the city in Roman Epirus, on the western coast of Greece. Titus must have traveled north into Dalmatia following this rendezvous with Paul (2 Tim 4:10). See note on Tit 1:4.

3:13 Zenas the lawyer and Apollos: Possibly the bearers of this letter. The former is otherwise unknown in the NT, but the latter was a renowned convert from Alexandria, Egypt (Acts 18:24–26), who later ministered in Corinth (Acts 19:1; 1 Cor 1:12; 3:4–6).

3:15 Grace be with you all: Paul is addressing the entire community, not just Titus. The intent is to show the Cretans that Titus is Paul's official representative on the island. No one who reads the letter will doubt that he is commissioned by the apostle to teach, organize, and discipline with full authority (2:15). Paul employs a similar strategy on Timothy's behalf in 1 Tim 6:21 and 2 Tim 4:22.

STUDY QUESTIONS
Titus

Chapter 1

For understanding

1. **1:4.** Who is Titus? Where do we learn about him in the New Testament? What may the expression "my true child" suggest to the reader? In the Bible, with what is spiritual fatherhood connected?
2. **1:5.** What is known about Paul's and Titus' evangelization of Crete? What does the duty of appointing elders indicate about Titus himself? How are the titles "elder" and "bishop" used at this stage of the Church's development?
3. **1:6.** Why did the early Church rule that a bishop should be married only once in his lifetime? For whom does Paul grant—and refuse to grant—a concession with respect to remarriage?
4. **1:15.** What does the expression "to the pure" imply? What does Paul insist on regarding the purity of Christians? What is it important to understand that he is *not* saying?

For application

1. **1:7-8.** Why is it especially important for those who have a vocation to the ordained ministry to strive after virtue and holiness? Who else is called to live virtuous and holy lives? In what areas can you become more virtuous and holy?
2. **1:9-10.** How would you recognize an "insubordinate" teacher of the faith? To whom must such a person be subordinate, at least in the teaching presented?
3. **1:11.** Many complain today that insubordinate teachers are not "silenced" by their bishops. How would you advise a person who is upset that a dissident teacher is apparently allowed to continue teaching? Have you ever considered praying for such teachers rather than criticizing them?
4. **1:15.** How do you understand the saying "To the pure all things are pure"? Why is this not a license to do whatever one wants? Since Paul immediately qualifies the proverb by adding, "To the corrupt and unbelieving, nothing is pure", how would you place this proverb in the context of the proper formation of conscience?

Chapter 2

For understanding

1. **2:1-10.** To whom is Titus instructed to give moral counsel in these verses? With what expectation does Paul associate faith and life? In effect, then, what does Paul want of Cretan believers?
2. **2:9.** Since slavery was an accepted institution in Roman society, what did Paul seek to accomplish in commenting on it? What did he generally stress? In this verse, what does Paul imply about the dependability and service of slaves?
3. **2:11-14.** What is the purpose of these verses? On what does Paul place emphasis?
4. **2:14.** Where does the expression "a people of his [God's] own" come from? How do Exodus and Deuteronomy use these words? Since the persistence of sin and weakness prevented Israel from fulfilling its vocation under the Old Covenant, what did Christ come to do?

For application

1. **2:2-3.** Why might Paul be concerned to bid older persons to be "temperate, serious, sensible, sound in faith, in love, and in steadfastness" as well as temperate in speech? What issues do older adults face that might tempt them to be the opposite?
2. **2:6.** What aspects of self-control have you found most challenging? Why is self-control so necessary for a Christian (not to mention a mature adult)? Why do you think self-control is under such attack in our society?

3. **2:9–10.** Have you ever been tempted to steal from your employer or company? How have you resisted? If you have stolen anything, what have you done to make restitution? What should you do when you realize that others are stealing?

4. **2:11–14.** What is the difference between this vision of life in the world and a self-repressed severity? What does it mean to be both "sober, upright, and godly", on the one hand, and joyful, on the other?

Chapter 3

For understanding

1. **3:1.** What is Paul telling Titus about the attitude Christians need to take toward public life? What must the saints be (besides holy)?

2. **Word Study: Regeneration (3:5).** To what does the Greek word for *regeneration* refer? How do extrabiblical writers use the word? To what does Paul link the idea here? What is he saying, in effect?

3. **3:10–11.** What do these two verses present? What is Titus supposed to do, and in what order?

4. **3:15.** By addressing the entire community, not just Titus, what is Paul trying to show the Cretan Church? What is Titus' commission?

For application

1. **3:1–2.** How does Paul's ideal of good civic behavior enhance the tone of public life?

2. **3:3–7.** According to these verses, why does God our Savior pay attention to your situation? How does he accomplish what he wants? What is his purpose?

3. **3:8–9.** Can you think of times when it is more appropriate and effective to teach sound doctrine by "good deeds" rather than by direct conversation that is likely to lead to "stupid controversies"? How might you avoid controversy without dispensing with all discussion of religion?

BOOKS OF THE BIBLE

THE OLD TESTAMENT

Gen	Genesis
Ex	Exodus
Lev	Leviticus
Num	Numbers
Deut	Deuteronomy
Josh	Joshua
Judg	Judges
Ruth	Ruth
1 Sam	1 Samuel
2 Sam	2 Samuel
1 Kings	1 Kings
2 Kings	2 Kings
1 Chron	1 Chronicles
2 Chron	2 Chronicles
Ezra	Ezra
Neh	Nehemiah
Tob	Tobit
Jud	Judith
Esther	Esther
Job	Job
Ps	Psalms
Prov	Proverbs
Eccles	Ecclesiastes
Song	Song of Solomon
Wis	Wisdom
Sir	Sirach (Ecclesiasticus)
Is	Isaiah
Jer	Jeremiah
Lam	Lamentations
Bar	Baruch
Ezek	Ezekiel
Dan	Daniel
Hos	Hosea
Joel	Joel
Amos	Amos
Obad	Obadiah
Jon	Jonah
Mic	Micah
Nahum	Nahum
Hab	Habakkuk
Zeph	Zephaniah
Hag	Haggai
Zech	Zechariah
Mal	Malachi
1 Mac	1 Maccabees
2 Mac	2 Maccabees

THE NEW TESTAMENT

Mt	Matthew
Mk	Mark
Lk	Luke
Jn	John
Acts	Acts of the Apostles
Rom	Romans
1 Cor	1 Corinthians
2 Cor	2 Corinthians
Gal	Galatians
Eph	Ephesians
Phil	Philippians
Col	Colossians
1 Thess	1 Thessalonians
2 Thess	2 Thessalonians
1 Tim	1 Timothy
2 Tim	2 Timothy
Tit	Titus
Philem	Philemon
Heb	Hebrews
Jas	James
1 Pet	1 Peter
2 Pet	2 Peter
1 Jn	1 John
2 Jn	2 John
3 Jn	3 John
Jude	Jude
Rev	Revelation (Apocalypse)